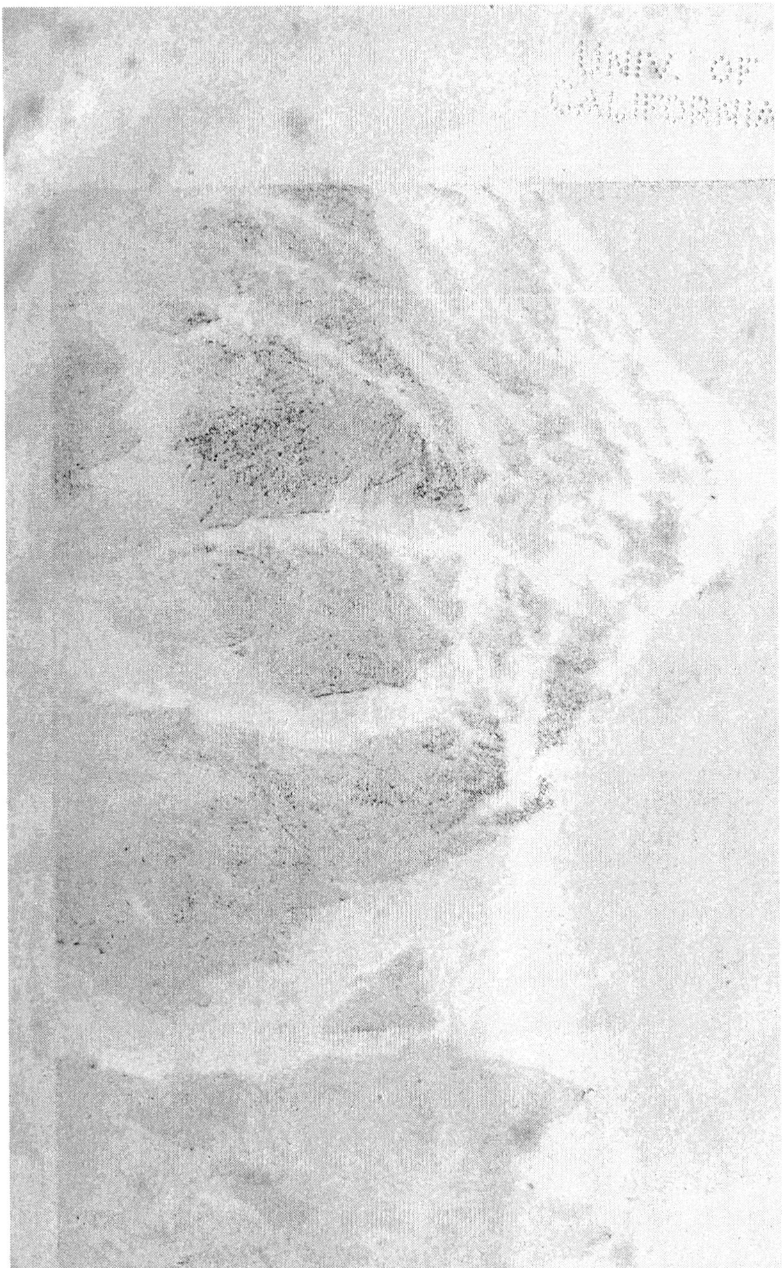
UNIV. OF
CALIFORNIA

THE SUMMIT OF THE AIGUILLE VERTE.

SWISS PICTURES

DRAWN WITH PEN AND PENCIL.

BY THE

REV. SAMUEL MANNING, LL.D.,

AUTHOR OF

"THOSE HOLY FIELDS," "SPANISH PICTURES," AND "ITALIAN PICTURES."

WITH ILLUSTRATIONS BY MR. WHYMPER, AND OTHERS.

A New and Enlarged Edition.

LONDON:

THE RELIGIOUS TRACT SOCIETY,

56, PATERNOSTER ROW; 65, ST. PAUL'S CHURCHYARD;

AND 164, PICCADILLY.

BRIGHTON: 31, WESTERN ROAD. MANCHESTER: 100, CORPORATION STREET.

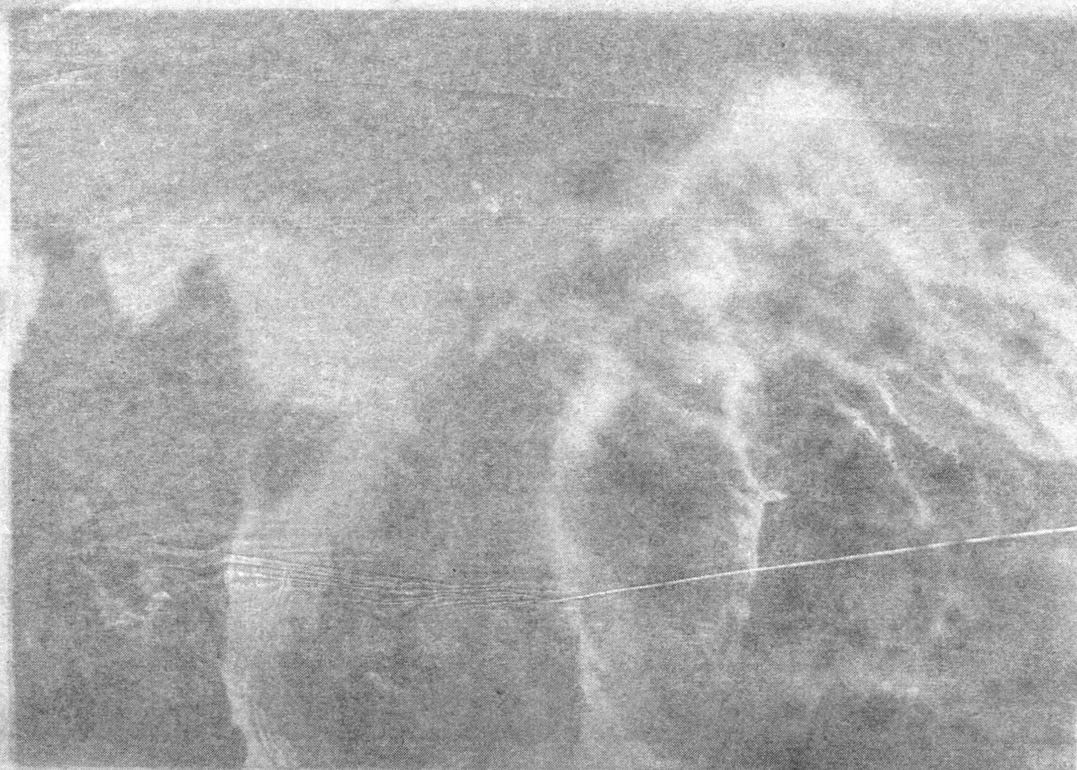

THE SUMMIT OF THE AIGUILLE VERTE.

SWISS PICTURES

DRAWN WITH PEN AND PENCIL.

BY THE

REV. SAMUEL MANNING, LL.D.,

AUTHOR OF

"THOSE HOLY FIELDS," "SPANISH PICTURES," AND "ITALIAN PICTURES."

WITH ILLUSTRATIONS BY MR. WHYMPER, AND OTHERS.

A New and Enlarged Edition.

LONDON:

THE RELIGIOUS TRACT SOCIETY;

56, PATERNOSTER ROW; 65, ST. PAUL'S CHURCHYARD;

AND 164, PICCADILLY.

BRIGHTON: 31, WESTERN ROAD. MANCHESTER: 100, CORPORATION STREET.

"The feeding of the rivers and the purifying of the winds are the least of the services appointed to the hills. To fill the thirst of the human heart with the beauty of God's working,—to startle its lethargy with the deep and pure agitation of astonishment—are their higher missions. They are as a great and noble architecture; first giving shelter, comfort, and rest; and covered also with mighty sculpture and painted legend."

Ruskin.

LONDON: PRINTED BY WILLIAM CLOWES AND SONS.

CONSULTING MURRAY.

CONTENTS.

Eastern Switzerland and the Rhine.

The Forest Cantons.

THE SIMPLON ROAD AND THE SWISS-ITALIAN LAKES.

THE MONTE ROSA DISTRICT.

THE BERNESE OBERLAND.

THE MONT BLANC DISTRICT.

WESTERN SWITZERLAND.

CHÂLETS NEAR SEPEY.

THE mountains of this glorious land
  Are conscious beings to mine eye,
When at the break of day they stand
  Like giants, looking through the sky,
To hail the sun's unrisen car,
  That gilds their diadems of snow;
While one by one, as star by star,
  Their peaks in ether glow.

Their silent presence fills my soul,
  When, to the horizontal ray,
The many-tinctured vapours roll
  In evanescent wreaths away,
And leave them naked on the scene,
  The emblems of eternity,
The same as they have ever been,
  And shall for ever be!

And O ye everlasting hills!
  Buildings, of God not made with hands,
Whose word performs whate'er He wills,
  Whose word, though ye shall perish, stands.
Can there be eyes that look on you,
  Till tears of rapture make them dim,
Nor in His works the Maker view,
  Then lose His works in Him?

By me, when I behold Him not,
  Or love Him not when I behold,
Be all I ever knew forgot:
  My pulse stand still, my heart grow cold;
Transformed to ice, 'twixt earth and sky,
  On yonder cliff my form be seen,
That all may ask, but none reply,
  What my offence hath been!

MONTGOMERY.

EASTERN SWITZERLAND AND THE RHINE.

WILD LIFE IN THE ALPS.

EASTERN SWITZERLAND AND THE RHINE.

BELGIUM AND THE RHINE—HEIDELBERG—SCHAFFHAUSEN—CONSTANCE AND JOHN HUS—ZURICH—EINSIEDELN—ST. GALL AND APPENZELL—THE GRISONS—HEAD WATERS OF THE RHINE—THE VIA MALA—THE ENGADINE AND PIZ LANGUARD.

SIR JOHN MANDEVILLE begins his chronicle of travel and adventure by saying, "He that will pass over the sea to go to the city of Jerusalem may go many ways, both by sea and land, according to the country that he cometh from: many ways come to one end. But you must not expect that I shall tell you all the towns and cities and castles that men shall go by, for then should I make too long a tale." The quaint old chronicler's words apply to Switzerland as well as to Jerusalem. The possible variations of route, each of which has its advocates and its advantages, are almost innumerable. That by Belgium and the Rhine has always seemed to me decidedly the best; for those tourists, at least, who have a few days to spare by the way. As the time occupied in transit is of little consequence to those who travel in their easy-chairs, let us at once decide upon this route.

What a delicious change, to break loose from the noise and bustle of English life, and lounge away a summer's afternoon in some sleepy old Flemish town, where "tall houses with quaint gables" lead the thoughts back to the days of Burgundian dukes and the stout brewers and cloth-workers of Ghent who "made their chivalry to skip."

Everything tells the tourist that he has left England far behind him; and with it, too, he seems to have left the nineteenth century, and to have passed back through half a dozen generations since he stepped ashore a few hours ago. Even the railroads, though made, to a great extent, by English hands and by English capital, have a strange, foreign look about them: if in nothing else, in the long, melancholy avenues of poplars that stretch across the country in all directions, and the women who have taken the place of pointsmen and gatekeepers.

Jaded with a year's hard toil of hand or brain, what a luxury it is to lie under the awning of a Rhine steamer, and let the scenery glide past one. Castled crags, vine-clad hills, white-walled towns, come and go as if under the

CANAL AND BELFRY AT BRUGES.

spell of some mighty magician. As you recline there, with the unwonted and delicious sense of having nothing to do, they come up to be looked at, and slip away, each with its legend of the storied past shedding a halo of romance around the picturesque beauty of the present.

Shall we linger for a day or two amongst the old-world cities and villages which line the banks of the noble river? Not a few of them have traditions and ruins which go back to the days of Drusus, and which may serve to illustrate every subsequent cycle of European history. Here Roman and Goth and Vandal, Gaul and Hun, have fought and died. There Charlemagne has left his mark. Templars held their consistories in this ruined keep. Noble and royal damsels pined in the seclusion of yonder nunnery. "On the right," says

THE LURLIE ROCK.

Lord Lytton, "rises the once imperial city of Boppart. In no journey of similar length do you meet with such striking instances of the mutability of power. To find, as in the Memphian Egypt, a city sunk into a heap of desolate ruins, the hum, the roar, the mart of nations, hushed into the silence of the ancestral tombs, is less humbling to our human vanity than to mark, as along the Rhine, the kingly city dwindled into the humble town or the dreary village—decay without its grandeur, change without the awe of its solitude. On the site on which Drusus raised his Roman tower, and the kings of the Franks their palaces, trade now dribbles in tobacco-pipes, and transforms into an excellent cotton factory the antique nunnery of Königsberg."

Amongst the ruined castles which "frown o'er the dark and winding Rhine," that of Rheinfels is one of the largest and most imposing. It rises to a height of three hundred and fifty feet over the little village beneath, topping the modern roofs and

STOLZENFELS.

chimneys with a crowd of broken towers and ramparts, jagged and grey and hoary. The whole appears like a town with a mere sediment of life still lingering in its lowest level, as if the part which skirted the stream were kept from decay by contact with the quickening waters of the river, while all above was dry and stiff with the paralysis of age.

BOPPART.

Few would travel by this route without turning aside to Heidelberg, whose castle well deserves the praise of being "the noblest wreck of German grandeur." The ruins, the surrounding mountains, the lovely valley, and the river winding along so placidly, all seem made for each other, and "each gives each a double charm."

But we shall never reach Switzerland at all if we lounge up every charming valley, or loiter on the banks of every winding river, or stop to listen to all the echoes of a romantic past. Indeed the danger of choosing this route is that

RHEINFELS.

the temptations to linger on the journey are so numerous and so strong that it is almost impossible to resist them. Every city has its history, every ruin its legend. Frankfort, and Spires, and Worms, are eloquent of Luther and the Reformation, and their histories stretch back to the Nieblungen-Lied, and the days of Alaric and Attila. Turning eastward, the Schwartzwald, the Taunus, the Odenwald, invite us to climb their pine-clad slopes, or penetrate their gloomy glens. But we must hasten on to our destination, where the Rhine will again meet us, no longer a German, but a Swiss river.

Traversing the Black Forest by the Höllenthal and the Himmelreich, we enter Switzerland at Schaffhausen. The town itself deserves and will repay a visit from the lovers of mediæval architecture. The walls, the gates, the halls of the old Guilds or Zünfte, the projecting gables, carved and painted in the quaintest fashion, compete in point of picturesqueness with those of Belgium or Germany. It is the Falls of the Rhine, however, which form the great attraction of Schaffhausen. The river, which is here about three hundred feet in breadth, plunges over the black rocks with a tremendous and deafening roar. The mass of water is greater than that of any other cataract in Europe. But it lacks height and suddenness. It is a rapid rather than a waterfall.

Is it possible to describe a waterfall? Can words represent that wonderful combination of monotony with intense tumultuous motion which constitutes its charm? If success is possible, Mr. Ruskin has attained it in his description of the Falls of the Rhine. "Stand for half an hour," he says, "beside the Fall of Schaffhausen, on the north side, where the rapids are long, and watch how the vault of water first bends, unbroken, in pure polished velocity, over the arching rocks at the brow of the cataract, covering them with a dome of crystal twenty feet thick, so swift that its motion is unseen except when a foam-globe

HEIDELBERG.

from above darts over it like a falling star; and how the trees are lighted above it under all their leaves at the instant that it breaks into foam; and how all the hollows of that foam burn with green fire like so much shattering chrysoprase; and how, ever and anon, startling you with its white flash, a jet of spray leaps hissing out of the fall, like a rocket, bursting in the wind and driven away in dust, filling the air with light; and how, through the curdling wreaths of the wrestling, crashing abyss below, the blue of the water, paled by the foam in its body, shows purer than the sky through white rain-cloud; while the shuddering

THE FALLS OF THE RHINE, SCHAFFHAUSEN.

iris stoops in tremulous stillness over all, fading and flushing alternately through the choking spray and shattered sunshine, hiding itself at last amongst the thick golden leaves which toss to and fro in sympathy with the wild water; their dripping masses lifted at intervals, like sheaves of loaded corn, by some stronger gush from the cataract, and bowed again upon the mossy rocks as its roar dies away; the dew gushing from their thick branches through drooping clusters of emerald herbage, and sparkling in white threads along the dark rocks of the shore, feeding the lichens which chase and chequer them with purple and silver."

CONSTANCE.

A short and interesting ride, either by railway or steamer, brings us to Constance—a decayed city, the population of which has dwindled from forty thousand to seven thousand. It owes its fame to the great council which met here A.D. 1414, at which one hundred thousand persons are said to have assembled. John Hus, summoned before this council to answer the charge of heresy, manfully declared his faith in Jesus, and sealed his testimony with his blood. He was confined in a dark and loathsome dungeon under the Dominican convent on the shore of the lake. The walls of his cell were saturated with water, which stood in pools on the floor. Only for a short period of each day was he able to read, when a ray of light struggled through an aperture in the roof of his prison. The rest of his time was passed in almost total darkness. Ecclesiastical history records few more touching scenes than that when Hus, condemned to die, fell upon his knees, like Stephen, the proto-martyr, and prayed, "O Lord God, I beseech thee, for thy mercy's sake, to pardon all my enemies. Thou knowest that I have been unjustly accused and condemned; but do thou forgive them this sin." This prayer was greeted with scornful

HUS'S MONUMENT.

laughter by the men on whose behalf it was offered. They heaped upon him reproaches of every kind, and denounced him as a second Judas. He bore all with the utmost meekness, saying, "I place all my confidence and hope in God my Saviour. I know that he will not take from me the cup of salvation; but by his grace I shall drink it to-day in his kingdom." So it proved. He was led forth to the stake, and there breathed his last in words of prayer and praise. The house in which he lodged, the minster in which he was tried, the spot where the stake was fixed, and that at which his ashes were cast into the Rhine, are still pointed out. A mass of rock, upon which his name is inscribed, near the site of his martyrdom, forms a fitting monument to his memory.

JOHN HUS IN PRISON.

From an old Painting in the possession of the Rev. W. Blackley, M.A.

Zurich, about thirty-five miles from Schaffhausen, has little to detain the tourist. The scenery in the neighbourhood and along the banks of its lake though pleasing, seldom rises above prettiness. To grandeur or sublimity it has no claim. But the English Protestant cannot fail to look with interest upon a spot so memorable in the history of the Reformation. Zurich has always afforded a refuge to those "set for the defence of the gospel." Even in the pre-Reformation period, Arnold of Brescia fled thither, pursued by papal vengeance. Here too Zwingle proclaimed the great truths of the gospel. In the venerable

ZURICH CATHEDRAL.

cathedral, on New Year's Day, 1519, he entered upon his ministry with these words, "It is to Christ that I desire to lead you; to Christ, the true source of salvation. His divine word is the only food that I wish to set before your hearts and souls." Here Farel and his fellow-labourers in the same glorious work had a rallying-point. Here too the Marian exiles, John Knox, Miles Coverdale, Anthony Gilby, and others, found more than a shelter, they found a welcome and a home. Of all these men and their works, relics are treasured in the museum of the city, together with some touching letters of the beautiful but unfortunate Lady Jane Grey.

Zwingle, before his election to the Cathedral Church of Zurich, had been priest at Einsiedeln, which lies some miles to the south, near the other end of the lake. The Abbey of Einsiedeln was long the richest, as it is still the most frequented pilgrimage-church in Europe. It has been estimated that not fewer than one hundred and fifty thousand pilgrims visit it annually; the numbers, however, are gradually diminishing. These come from all parts of Europe. Dr. Beattie makes the almost incredible statement, that he met there an aged peasant-woman, a hundred and eight years old, who had walked the whole way from the remotest corners of Normandy, in performance of a vow to the Virgin

EINSIEDELN.

of the Swiss mountains. During the pilgrimage season the steamers on the Lake of Zurich are crowded with devotees in the costume of almost every nationality in Catholic Christendom. The object of adoration is an ugly black doll, dressed in gold brocade, and glittering with jewels. The walls of the church are covered with votive offerings—rude paintings, wax figures, crutches—suspended in fulfilment of vows, or in acknowledgment of deliverance. An inscription offers a plenary indulgence to the pilgrim—*Hic est plena remissio peccatorum à culpâ et à panâ.* It was here, in the midst of dense superstition and blind idolatry, that Zwingle began his ministry and startled the crowds of pilgrims by declaring that "Christ *alone* saves, and he saves *everywhere.*"

BASLE.

"Do not imagine," he said, "that God is in this temple more than in any part of creation. Whatever be the country in which you dwell, God is around you, and hears you, as well as at Our Lady's of Einsiedeln. Jesus Christ is the only oblation, the only sacrifice, the only way."

Intimately associated with Zurich in the history of the Reformation was Basle. Here Erasmus waged war with the papacy, "sapping a solemn creed with solemn sneer." Here Zwingle, Œcolampadius, and their companions constantly met for consultation and mutual encouragement. Here the restless Farel, driven out from France, found a refuge from persecution, and waged a ceaseless and fiery war against the papal Antichrist. Hither, too, many of the Marian exiles fled—

"Scattering, like birds escaped the fowler's net,
They seek with timely flight a foreign strand;
Most happy, reassembled in a land
By dauntless Luther freed, could they forget
Their country's woes."

Basle has always held an important place in the religious history of Switzerland. It still forms a centre of evangelical and missionary activity, from which are sent out some of the most faithful, diligent, and successful labourers for Christ amongst the heathen.

Here, as everywhere, the Rhine is beautiful. If it lacks the picturesque beauty of its course between Mayence and Bonn, or the wild savage grandeur, the glaciers and the snow-peaks, of its birth-place and early career, or the grand fury with which it plunges over the falls at Schaffhausen, it has yet a charm of its own. Standing upon the bridge, or at the windows of the *Trois Rois,* and looking down into the deep, broad stream as it rushes past, one gains an impressive sense of resistless strength and exhaustless fulness. In no other part of its course does it fill an ampler channel or roll along with more impetuous rapidity. It enters the Lake of Constance turbid with the impurities of the glacier torrents which feed it. It emerges crystalline in purity, and deliciously green in colour. Well may Longfellow exclaim: "O the pride of the German heart in this noble river! And right it is, for of all the rivers of this beautiful earth there is none so beautiful as this. There is hardly a league of its whole course which boasts not of its peculiar charms. But I will not attempt to describe the Rhine; it would make this chapter too long; and to do it well one should write like a king, and his language should flow onward royally with breaks and dashes like the waters of that royal river, and antique, quaint, and Gothic times be reflected in it."

The Rhine ceases to be navigable above the Lake of Constance. For some distance it forms the boundary between Switzerland and the Tyrol. On the Swiss side are the Cantons of St. Gall and Appenzell, which are amongst the most busy and prosperous in the Confederation. They are the principal seat of the Swiss muslin manufacture. The artistic skill displayed in the designs, and the excellence of the workmanship, have won for these productions a deserved celebrity. Appenzell is divided into two distinct districts, which are independent of each other. Outer Rhoden is Protestant in religion, and its inhabitants are almost entirely engaged in manufactures. They are thriving, industrious, and well-educated. Inner Rhoden remains to this day Roman Catholic, and is amongst the most backward and stagnant districts in Switzerland. "It is inhabited," says Rougemont, "by a population of lax morality, uncivilised and fierce, idle, and therefore poor."* The contrast between Protestant and Papal Switzerland—the prosperity and intelligence of the former, the poverty and ignorance of the latter—which strike every traveller in the country, are especially obvious here. It is impossible to pass from the one district to the other, or to compare their statistics, without being impressed by the influence of religion on the well-being of the people.

FEMALE COSTUMES IN APPENZELL.

Leaving the Canton of St. Gall, and following the course of the Rhine upward towards its source, we enter the Grisons. We are now approaching the head waters of the noble river whose course we are tracing from "its cradle in the snowy Alps to its grave in the sands of Holland." Its two confluents, the Hinter and the Vorder Rhein, unite at Reichenau, near the foot of the Splugen. Reichenau has a place in modern European history, from the fact that Louis Philippe found refuge here, as an exile, during the first fury of the French

* See *Catholic and Protestant Nations compared.* By Napoleon Roussel, p. 174. He cites a large number of witnesses, many of them enthusiastic Romanists, in support of the statement in the text.

Revolution. His rank was unknown to the villagers, who only recognised him as Monsieur Chabot, teacher of French, mathematics, and history in the Burgomaster Tscharmer's school, of which M. Jost was head-master. He arrived on foot, in the year 1793, a stick in his hand and a bundle on his back. For eight months he diligently discharged the duties of his humble calling, and is said to have won the affection and respect of both masters and scholars, only one of whom suspected his secret. The lives of few men have been marked by stranger vicissitudes than those of Louis Philippe and his successor on the throne of France. Louis Napoleon, like his predecessor, spent part of his life in obscurity and exile in Switzerland, and the home of both was near the banks of the Rhine.

PEASANTS OF EASTERN SWITZERLAND.

The main point of interest in the Hinter Rhein is the Via Mala. The noble river is here in its infancy. Compressed between the rocks which enclose its bed, it is scarcely wider than a rivulet, but the chasm which it has cleft for itself is one of the most imposing and awe-inspiring gorges in the world. The valley seems to be absolutely closed up by an impenetrable barrier of rock, and it is only on a near approach that a narrow rift is discovered, out of which the infant river bursts. Entering this gorge, the mountains on either side rise higher and higher, the chasm becomes narrower, far below the raging torrent roars and thunders in its rocky bed, sometimes at a depth so great as to be almost inaudible; a narrow strip of sky is all that can be descried overhead, and the ravine beneath lies in impenetrable darkness. In some places the cliffs on either hand rise to a height of sixteen hundred feet. "You enter this savage pass from a world of beauty, from the sunlit vale of Domschleg, under the old Etruscan

VIA MALA.

castle of Realt, spiked in the cliff like a war-club, four hundred feet above you, and totally inaccessible on every side save one, and are plunged at once into a scene of such concentrated and deep sublimity, such awe-inspiring grandeur, such overwhelming power, that you advance slowly and solemnly, as if every crag were a supernatural being. The road is carried with great daring along the perpendicular face of crags, cut from the rock where no living thing could have scaled the mountain, and sometimes it completely overhangs the

PIZ LANGUARD.

abyss, a thousand feet above the raging torrent. Now it pierces the rock, now it runs zigzag, now spans the gorge on a light dizzy bridge; now the mountains frown on each other like tropical thunder-clouds about to meet and discharge their artillery, and now you come upon mighty insulated crags, thrown wildly together, covered with fringes of moss and shrubbery, constituting masses of verdure. Nothing can be finer than the effect where you look through the ravine, as through a mighty perspective, with the Realt Castle hanging to the cliff at its mouth, and the sunny air and earth expanding in such contrast with the frowning gloom-invested tremendous passage behind you. We leaned over the parapet, and endeavoured to guess at the depth of the chasm. It was dizzy to look at. The tall black fir-forests on the mountain shelves, and the blasted pines on the inaccessible peaks, seemed to gaze gravely at us as if we had come unauthorised into a sanctuary of nature too deep and awful to be trodden by the foot of man."*

SOURCES OF THE RHINE.

At a few hours' distance the sources of the Rhine may be reached. Like most Swiss streams, they are fed by the drainage of glaciers.

Within the last few years the Engadine, in the eastern part of the Grisons, has risen into popularity with tourists—and most deservedly so. Until the railway was completed to Chur, this district lay so far out of the line of the regular Swiss round, and was so difficult of access, that it could be visited only by those who were prepared to "rough it." The few who were able and willing to deviate from the beaten track were abundantly repaid by finding themselves in a region little known, but which combined the grandeur of Switzerland with the picturesqueness of the Tyrol. Now St. Moritz and Pontresina have become almost English settlements. In addition to the sublimity and beauty of the scenery, and the exquisite purity of the air, mineral springs, which are deemed of great efficacy in many complaints, attract crowds of invalids.

* *Wanderings of a Pilgrim*, by Cheever.

One of the chief attractions of the Engadine is the ascent of Piz Languard. The point from which the ascent is made is the village of Pontresina, about two hours' walk from St. Moritz, lying on the high road to the Bernina Pass. Its position is so favourable for both mountain and glacier excursions, that it has become to the south-east what Chamouni is to the south-west of Switzerland. Piz Languard rises to the height of 10,714 feet; but, as Pontresina itself is nearly 6000 feet above the level of the sea, the actual climb is something less than 5000 feet; and, owing to the peculiar shape of the mountain, the summit is easily accessible. The ascent commences close behind the church at the south end of the village, and for an hour, or an hour and a quarter, is somewhat steep and difficult. But the mule path is broad, and passes by zigzags through pines and larches fringed by rhododendrons. Somewhat suddenly, the path emerges upon almost level pastures, where the flocks of the Bergamasque shepherds may generally be seen. What is termed the Valley of Languard is soon seen, reaching right up to the base of the pyramid which forms the summit of Piz Languard. This valley is of a singularly wild and desolate character, presenting scarcely anything to the view but loose stones and rocks. Traversing this in about three quarters of an hour, you stand at the commencement of the final climb. Horses can come thus far; but whoever would enjoy the glorious scene from the summit must here dismount and trust himself to his own feet. The first look is certainly not inviting. A sharp precipitous pyramid rises up out of the valley just traversed, and the pathway lies more or less on one of the angles of the pyramid. The consequence is, that there are several parts of the ascent from which you can look down seemingly immeasurable depths on either side. There is, however, no danger. Pressing steadily on, three-quarters of an hour will suffice to conquer the difficulty, and to place you on the summit. As may be supposed from its

VALLEY IN THE ENGADINE.

contour, the summit is very confined, not affording space for more than from twenty to thirty persons. But once there, every other thought will be swallowed up in the magnificence of the prospect that stretches out to the horizon on every side. East, west, north, and south, a bewildering succession of snow-clad peaks meet the eye; and it will be some time before the spectator can descend to the particulars of the scene, for the panorama comprises the snow-clad peaks of East Switzerland, Monte Rosa, the Tödi, the Adamello-group, and the Zug Spitz, the whole resembling a gigantic relief-map. Having feasted his eyes on

THE ORTLER SPITZ.

this wondrous vision, the spectator may now note some of its special features. Let him turn to the south, and he stands face to face with the Bernina chain, and looks down upon the magnificent Morteratsch Glacier flowing from its heights. Turning a little to the east, he sees the Bernina Pass winding its way like a narrow thread over into Italy; on the summit he will notice two lakes, called the Black and the White, from the colour of their waters. The narrow strip which separates them is the water-shed; for the Black flows on this side to the River Inn, and the White on that to the Adda. Looking still farther to the east, across into the Tyrol, he sees the huge Ortler Spitz, and the

Oetzthaler Ferner, glistering with their snow and ice in the rays of the sun. To the south-west, though at least sixty miles off, Monte Rosa rises up like a vast white cliff; and beyond that, it is averred, Mont Blanc can be seen. The guide said it could be detected; but to the question, "Können *Sie* es sehen?" answered, "Nein." West, the Bernese Alps glow in all their brightness; while, in the north, chain after chain of well-known mountains are beheld. The effect on the mind of such a stupendous scene is almost overwhelming; for, with one exception, there is no contrast. It is all mountains in the picture, excepting St. Moritz, with its green lake, and two neighbouring villages, which lie, like a child's toy-garden, away down in the distant valley.

CAUB AND PFALZ.

THE FOREST CANTONS.

IN THE PINE FOREST.

THE FOREST CANTONS.

LUCERNE—THE RIGI—SUNDAY ON THE RIGI—LAKE OF LUCERNE—ENGELBERG—THE ST. GOTHARD AND DEVIL'S BRIDGE.

THE adjacent Cantons of Lucerne, Schwytz, Unterwalden, and Uri, are grouped together as the Forest Cantons. They enclose between them the Lake of Lucerne, or, as the Swiss call it, the Vierwaldstädter-See, the Lake of the Four Forest Cantons. The shores of the lake abound in scenery of transcendent beauty and grandeur. The district is full of stirring historical associations and romantic legends; for it was here that the great battles of Swiss freedom were fought and won. It is the country of Fürst and Stauffhacher, Arnold von Winkelried and William Tell, of Sempach and Morgarten, and Grutli.

A railway ride of two or three hours (fifty-seven and a half miles) brings the traveller from Basle to Lucerne. The River Reuss here rushes from the lake with extraordinary velocity and force. The curious old bridges by which the clear blue torrent is crossed form the most characteristic feature of the city. Two of them are of great length. They are roofed and partially enclosed. The inner sides are ornamented with rude but vigorous paintings. In some, the narratives of the Old and New Testament

BRIDGE OF LUCERNE.

are depicted; in others, the most important events in Swiss history; here you have the legends of the patron saints of the city, and there a Dance of Death. In the last, which forms the decoration of the Sprener Brücke, there is a grim humour and quaint truthfulness which are very impressive. These bridges form a most agreeable lounge on a summer's afternoon. The roof with its projecting eaves affords ample shade; the ice-cold river rushes beneath, clear as crystal, swift as a mountain torrent. When the eye is wearied with looking at the pictures, no more agreeable rest can be desired than to lean over the parapet and gaze down into the crystalline depths below, or out over the lovely lake to the mighty mountains beyond.

The monument to the memory of the faithful Swiss Guard, who fell on the 10th of August, 1792, while attempting to defend the royal family of France from the attack of a revolutionary mob, is carved on the face of a rock in the outskirts of the city. It is from a design by Thorwaldsen, and represents a colossal lion, dying of his wounds, endeavouring, even in the agonies of death, to protect a shield bearing the fleur-de-lys. It is scarcely exaggeration when Mr. Ball speaks of it as "perhaps the most appropriate and touching monument in existence."

The great excursion from Lucerne is to the Rigi. Innumerable attempts have been made to describe the view from the summit; perhaps that by Cheever is one of the best:—

"It was the 6th of September, and the most perfectly beautiful morning that can be imagined. At a quarter-past three the stars were reigning supreme in the heavens, with just enough of the old moon left to make a trail of light in the shape of a little silver boat among them. But speedily the horizon began to redden over the eastern range of mountains, and then the dawn stole on in such a succession of deepening tints, that nothing but the hues of the preceding sunset could be more beautiful. But there is this great difference between the sunrise and sunset, that the hues of sunset are every moment deepening as you look upon them, until they fade into the darkness, while those of the sunrise gradually fade into the light of day. It is difficult to say which process is the more beautiful; for if you could make everything stand still around you, if you could stereotype or stay the process for an hour, you could not tell whether it were the morning dawn or the evening twilight.

MONUMENT TO THE SWISS GUARD.

TELL'S CHAPEL, LAKE OF LUCERNE.

"A few long, thin stripes of fleecy cloud lay motionless above the eastern horizon, like layers of silver lace, dipped first in crimson, then in gold, then in pink, then lined with an ermine of light, just as if the moon had been lengthened in soft furrows along the sky. This scene in the east attracts every eye at first, but it is not here that *the* glory of the view is to be looked for. This glory is in that part of the horizon on which the sun first falls, as he struggles up behind the mountains to flood the world with light. And the reason why it is so glorious is because, long before you call it sunrise in the east, he lights up in the west a range of colossal pyres, that look like blazing cressets kindled from the sky.

"The object most conspicuous as the dawn broke, and indeed the most sublimely beautiful, was the vast enormous range of the snowy mountains of the

ASCENDING THE RIGI.

Oberland, without spot or veil of cloud or mist to dim them; the Finsteraarhorn at the left, and the Jungfrau and Silberhorn at the right, peak after peak and mass after mass, glittering with a cold wintry whiteness in the grey dawn. Almost the exact half of the circumference of the horizon commanded before and behind in our view, was filled with these peaks and masses of snow and ice, then lower down the mountains of bare rock, and lower still the earth with mounds of verdure; and this section of the horizontal circumference, which is filled with the vast ranges of the Oberland Alps, being almost due west from the sun's first appearance, it is on their tops that the rising ray's first strike.

"This was the scene for which we watched, and it seems as if nothing in nature can ever again be so beautiful. It was as if an angel had flown round the horizon of mountain ranges, and lighted up each of their white pyramidal

THE RIGI AND KUSSNACHT.

points in succession, like a row of gigantic lamps burning with rosy fires. Just so the sun suddenly tipped the highest points and lines of the snowy outline, and then, descending lower on the body of the mountain, it was as if an invisible Omnipotent hand had taken them, and dipped the whole range in a glowing pink; the line between the cold snow untouched by the sunlight and the warm roseate hue above remaining perfectly distinct. This effect continued some minutes, becoming, up to a certain point, more and more beautiful.

"In truth no word was uttered when that scene became visible. Each person gazed in silence. It was as if we witnessed some supernatural revelation, where mighty spirits were the actors between earth and heaven. And yet a devout soul might have almost felt, seeing those fires kindled as on the altars of God made visible, as if it heard the voices of Seraphim crying, Holy, Holy, Holy is the Lord of Hosts, the whole earth is full of His glory! For, indeed, the vision was so radiant, so full of sudden, vast, and unimaginable beauty and splendour, that methinks a phalanx of the Sons of God, who might have been passing at that moment, could not have helped stopping and shouting for joy as on the morning of creation.

"This was the transient view, which, to behold, one might well undertake a voyage across the Atlantic;—of a glory and a beauty indescribable, and nowhere else in the world to be enjoyed, and here only in perfect weather. After these few moments, when the sun rose so high that the whole masses of snow upon the mountain ranges were lighted with the same rosy light, it grew rapidly fainter, till you could no longer distinguish the deep exquisite pink and rosy hues by means of their previous contrast with the cold white. Next the sun's rays fell upon the bare rocky peaks, where there was neither snow nor vegetation, making them shine like jasper, and next on the forests and soft grassy slopes, and so down into the deep bosom of the vales. The pyramidal shadow cast by the Rigi was most distinct and beautiful, but the atmospheric phenomenon of the Spectre of the Rigi was not visible.

PILATUS, LAKE OF LUCERNE.

"This amazing panorama is said to extend over a circumference of three hundred miles. In all this region, when the upper glory of the heavens and mountain-peaks has ceased playing, then, as the sun gets higher, forests, lakes, hills, rivers, trees, and villages, at first indistinct and grey in shadow, become flooded with sunshine, and almost seem floating up towards you.

"There was for us another feature of the view, constituting by itself one of the most novel and charming sights of Swiss scenery, but which does not always accompany the panorama from the Rigi, even in a fine morning. This was the soft smooth white body of mist, lying on most of the lakes and in the vales, a sea of mist, floating or rather brooding, like a white dove, over the landscape. The spots of land at first visible in the midst of it were just like islands half emerging to the view. It lay over the Bay of Kussnacht at our feet, like the white robe of an infant in the cradle, but the greater part of the Lake of Lucerne was sleeping quietly without it, as an undressed babe. Over the whole of the Lake of Zug the mist was at first motionless, but in the breath of the morning it began slowly to move altogether towards the west, disclosing the village of Arth and the verdurous borders of the lake, and then uncovering its deep sea-green waters, which reflected the lovely sailing shadows of the clouds as a mirror.

THE RIGI RAILWAY.

"Now the church bells began to chime under this body of mist, and voices from the invisible villages, mingled with the tinkle of sheep-bells, and the various stir of life awakening from sleep, came stilly up the mountain. And now some of the mountain peaks themselves began suddenly to be touched with fleeces of cloud, as if smoking with incense in morning worship. Detachments of mist begin also to rise from the lakes and valleys, moving from the main body up into the air. The villages, châlets, and white roads, dotting and threading the vast circumference of landscape, come next into view. And now on the Lake Zug you may see reflected the shadows of clouds that have risen from the surface, but are themselves below us."

The ascent of the Rigi has recently been facilitated, but at the same time vulgarised, by the construction of a railway. It will, of course, only be worked during the summer months, and will be exposed to serious risk of damage or

RAILWAY UP THE RIGI.

even destruction in the early spring from the melting snow, the rush of swollen torrents, and masses of falling rocks, which come thundering down with resistless force. The entire length of the railway is 17,500 Swiss feet, worked by engines of 120 horse-power. Much more enjoyable, if more fatiguing, was the old mode of ascent, on foot or horse-back, winding through pine-forests, or amongst masses of the *Nagelflue*, of which the mountain is composed.

Out of half a dozen visits to the Rigi Kulm, the one to which I look back

VITZNAU STATION ON THE RIGI, 1464 FEET ABOVE THE LEVEL OF THE SEA.

with most enjoyable feelings is a night ascent. An accident to the steamer on the lake had delayed us, so that the daylight was fading away when we landed. Most of the passengers went on to Lucerne. But I was familiar with the route; it was a brilliant evening; the moon was only just past the full, and would rise in a couple of hours; and, being very early in the season, we could depend upon finding accommodation on the summit. We therefore resolved to go on that night. Of course the people at the inn protested vehemently against so unheard-of a breach of precedent. "No horses could be had, the route was unsafe after nightfall, the hotel on the summit was crowded;" and they rehearsed a series of disasters to benighted travellers which would have terrified a tourist unversed in the manners and customs of Swiss hotel-keepers. But, as I was resolute in my determination to proceed, the difficulties vanished, and a few minutes after seven o'clock we were clattering along the stony street which leads from the village.

As soon as we got well away from the hotel our guides, who had previously confirmed all that the hotel-keeper had said as to the impossibilities and perils of the ascent, began, by more than usual gaiety and alacrity, to show the satisfaction which they really felt at this unexpected engagement.

For the first hour of the ascent we were in deep shadow. There was, indeed, no real danger; but there was sufficient appearance of it to give the zest of excitement to our journey. Of course as we were climbing the mountain side the moon was rising higher in the heavens, and by eight o'clock we could see the surrounding peaks lit up in a radiance which made the gloom in which we were moving the deeper by contrast. In a little while, turning a projecting corner, we came out upon a shoulder of the mountain, and found ourselves suddenly standing in a flood of intense white light. Below us was the lake flashing in the moonbeams. Round us stood the mountains, some in deep shadow, dotted over here and there by the lights of innumerable châlets; others were clear and distinct in the moonlight; overhead stretched a cloudless sky, with one planet and a star or two, uneclipsed by the moonbeams. We stood for some moments silent and spell-bound. The silence was at length broken by one of our party exclaiming, in the words of the psalmist, "O Lord, how manifold are Thy works! in wisdom hast Thou made them all." Taking out my pocket psalter, I read the viii. and the civ. psalms. We then joined in singing Addison's fine hymn, "The spacious firmament on high." Familiar as was the second verse, it seemed to become instinct with a new meaning and beauty, as sung under these circumstances:—

"Soon as the evening shades prevail,
The moon takes up the wondrous tale,
And nightly to the listening earth
Repeats the story of her birth;
Whilst all the stars that round her burn,
And all the planets in their turn,
Confirm the tidings as they roll,
And spread the truth from pole to pole."

We made many such halts in the course of the ascent, as new scenes of grandeur and beauty burst upon us. I shall never forget the weird effect of the crosses and rude carvings and paintings which line the mule-track. The coarseness of the execution was hidden by the glamour of the moonlight.

NIGHT ASCENT OF THE RIGI.

Stern Protestants as we were, we could not resist the solemn effect of these effigies of our Lord's "cross and passion."

When we reached the hotel on the summit, all was silent, save the baying of the watch-dogs. Everybody was in bed, and, if we may judge of the soundness of their sleep by the time it took to arouse them, they were very sound asleep indeed. At length, after knocking for about half an hour, the door was cautiously opened, and, after some parley, we succeeded in convincing the astonished garçon that we were bonâ fide travellers. Having hastily supped on some scraps of bread and cold meat, we went to bed.

Sunday morning opened without a cloud. The cold steely-grey of the eastern sky slowly brightened. Almost imperceptibly the wonderful panorama of mountain and lake and forest became visible. A faint flush of pink appeared on the horizon. The long line of snow-peak and ice-field began to glow with colour, in response to the growing radiance of the sky. Then silently and suddenly the great sun shot up, "as a bridegroom coming out of his chamber, and rejoicing as a strong man to run a race." Even the most thoughtless and frivolous of the party assembled on the platform that morning were impressed by the grandeur of the scene. And when a Lutheran pastor read aloud the xix. psalm in the grand old German version, there were few who did not seem to acknowledge "that the heavens declare the glory of God, and the firmament showeth His handy-work."

By eight o'clock breakfast was over, and all the guests save ourselves had departed. Not a little surprise was manifested when we declared our intention of remaining for the day. Of the thousands of travellers who ascend the Rigi during the season, probably not a dozen remain on the Kulm after breakfast; but we longed for a season of quiet retirement with God, and resolved to enjoy it on the summit. We arranged to spend a couple of hours in our own rooms, or in such solitude as each might prefer, and to meet for worship in a sheltered hollow a little way down the hill-side, which commanded a magnificent view of the Lake of Lucerne and the mountains of Uri. The hours went by with holy gladness. We worshipped God in the temple not made with hands, and could sympathise with all that James Hamilton has said, in "The Mount of Olives," of the sanctifying and solemnising effect of mountains. We seemed to be lifted up above the earth, and brought into conscious nearness to the skies.

It was with regret, almost with repugnance, that, as the afternoon passed away, we found our sabbath stillness invaded by the first stragglers of that great crowd of sight-seers who came flocking up the mountain to see the sunset. The shouts and songs that filled the air sounded like desecration. Not only the day but the place had been sacred. It had been to us "the house of God" and "the gate of heaven," and it seemed shocking that its sanctity should be thus rudely invaded.

As the hour of sunset came on, even this noisy crowd was hushed into silence. The shadows crept over the lakes and valleys and up the sides of the mountains, till the lower world was wrapped in gloom. The snow-peaks of the Bernese Oberland glowed in a crimson light, which slowly faded, till only a few of the highest pinnacles retained the ruddy flush. Then this too died out, and the mountains lay outstretched in the cold grey twilight like corpses from which the life had just departed.

The length of the Lake of Lucerne is about twenty-five English miles. "It is distinguished above every lake in Switzerland, perhaps in Europe, by the beauty and sublime grandeur of its scenery. It is hardly less interesting from the historical recollections connected with it. Its shores are a classic region—the sanctuary of liberty; on them took place those memorable events which gave freedom to Switzerland. Here the first confederacy was formed; and above all, its borders were the scene of the heroic deeds and signal vengeance of William Tell." Most readers will remember Rogers' lines:

ON THE LAKE OF LUCERNE.

"That sacred lake, withdrawn among the hills,
Its depth of waters flanked as with a wall
Built by the giant race before the Flood;
Where not a cross or chapel but inspires
Holy delight, lifting our thoughts to God. . . .
Who would not land in each and tread the ground,
Land where Tell leaped ashore, and climb to drink
Of the three hallowed fountains?"

The road along the eastern shores of the lake from Fluelen to Schwytz is one of the marvels of Swiss engineering. Somtimes it runs along the edge of the lake, then is lost to view in some dark, gloomy ravine, and presently reappears high up on the mountain side, scooped out of the perpendicular rock, and apparently overhanging the abyss. Looked at from below, the roadway can sometimes be scarcely seen. Vehicles and droves of cattle passing along it seem to cling like flies to the face of the cliff. Accidents, though rare, yet sometimes happen, and to fall from the dizzy height at which these Alpine roads often run, is, of course, fatal. An engraving from the original painting by the well-known Swiss artist Jenny, gives an impressive view of the scenery of this part of the lake, and the perils of the herdsmen.

BY THE LAKE OF LUCERNE.
From the original Painting by H. Jenny.

Leaving the lake, we proceed through Altorf, where Tell is said to have shot the apple from his son's head. A fountain, in the middle of the town, surmounted by his statue, marks the spot where the hero stood when taking his perilous aim; and a tower covered with rude frescoes occupies the place where the linden-tree grew to which the boy was bound. Wordsworth has some fine lines on the incident. But modern criticism affirms the whole affair to be a myth!

THE CHAISE-À-PORTEUR.

Proceeding along the valley of the Reuss, the road at first winds through a luxuriant region of orchards, and vineyards, and fertile meadows. The hills are clothed to their summits with richest verdure. The tinkling of cattle-bells is heard on every side. The ascent, though continuous, is so gradual as to be scarcely perceptible. But before many miles have been passed the scenery assumes more of an Alpine character. The vegetation becomes less rich. Forests of pine and fir take the place of walnut and beech. The valley contracts, and the huge mountain-peaks of Uri overhang it in savage grandeur.

ENGELBERG AND THE TITLIS.

Reaching Amsteg, a most interesting detour from the direct route to the St. Gothard may be made by taking the Surenen Pass to Engelberg, returning by the Susten. Supposing ladies to be of the party, the *chaise-à-porteur* may, not improbably, be put into requisition across the pass. This mode of conveyance is largely used in Switzerland by those who are unable to walk, or to endure the fatigue of riding. It is not a little surprising to see ladies, who, in England, would shrink from crossing a wooden bridge, even with a rail on either hand, borne in these crazy-looking vehicles, on the brink of unfathomable precipices, without a protest or a murmur.

THE DEVIL'S BRIDGE, ON THE ST. GOTHARD ROAD.

Engelberg is a little village at the junction of the Surenen and the Joch Passes. Its situation is very grand, embosomed in a deep broad valley at the foot of the "Snowy Titlis." The meadows around it are of the brightest green, encircled by belts of dark forest, seamed with cataracts, above which rise the mountains, some bleak and bare, some clad with verdure to the summit, and some reaching the region of perpetual snow. Over all, the Titlis stands in lonely grandeur.

Returning from Engelberg by the Sustenthal, the tourist regains the valley of the Reuss, at Wasen, and it is from this point that the grandest part of the St. Gothard route begins. A few miles bring him to the Devil's Bridge, a gorge which, for gloomy, savage grandeur, is scarcely, if at all, surpassed even by the Via Mala. "The granite rocks," says Dr. Beattie, "rise sheer and unbroken from the water's edge, and, as if bent on meeting overhead, threaten to obliterate the dismal path which the labour of ages has chiselled out of their flanks, or carried on arches along the brink of the torrent which foams far beneath. The deafening roar of the surge, as it struggles in savage conflict with the opposing rocks, and leaps and foams and thunders forth its song of triumph; the feeling of personal danger, the shaking of the low parapet where we stand, the beetling cliffs, along whose flanks the sheeted vapour floats in thin, transparent folds, the sudden gusts and currents of wind, caused by the rapidity of the torrent, the showers of spray alternately condensed and dissipated, or hurled in the spectator's face, burst upon the traveller with a novelty and power which baffle description. Never was there a theatre more congenial for the display of the wildest passions, or more in unison with every imaginable horror, than the Devil's Bridge." And horrors have not been wanting here. In the year 1799, the French, the Austrians, and the Russians, alternately drove each other out of this narrow gorge, and across the frail bridge which spans the raging torrent. During a whole month the tide of war ebbed to and fro, as the troops by turns attacked, repulsed, or were forced to retreat. Column after column was mowed down by the murderous fire, and swept into the horrible gulf, until the Reuss ran red with blood and was choked with corpses. At length victory declared against the French. They were driven down the valley to Altorf; and an inscription on the face of the living rock, at the summit of the pass—SUWARROW VICTOR—remains to attest the prowess of the Russian commander. Of that terrible conflict no other trace remains. The scars of battle have been effaced by the hand of Time. Nature has drawn her veil of verdure over the bloody scene. The peasant now pastures his flocks and herds in peace where the harvest of death was reaped.

THE SIMPLON ROAD

AND

THE SWISS-ITALIAN LAKES.

Drawn from Nature FISHING BY TORCHLIGHT ON THE SWISS LAKES. *by A. Mosengel.*

THE SIMPLON ROAD AND THE SWISS-ITALIAN LAKES.

ROUTES INTO THE LAKE DISTRICT—THE CONSTRUCTION OF THE SIMPLON ROAD—A WINTER ADVENTURE ON THE SIMPLON—ITALY—ITALIAN TOWNS—COMO, LUGANO, MAGGIORE, AND ORTA—THE BORROMEAN ISLANDS—STORM ON LAKE COMO—VENICE.

APPROACHING the lakes of Northern Italy from Switzerland, the route commonly taken is by one or other of the roads leading over the passes of the St. Gothard, the Simplon, or the Splugen. These roads have been constructed at immense cost, and are grandly engineered. Sometimes the path has been chiselled out of the face of a perpendicular rock, with an awful gulf on one side, and overhanging beetling cliffs on the other. Sometimes it has been tunnelled through the heart of the mountain, or flung at a dizzy height across a ravine, or carried in a series of zigzags up the side of a mountain, so steep that the chamois could scarcely climb it. At Gondo, on the Simplon, a cataract hurls itself sheer over the road* from the cliffs above, and plunges into the abyss below. At Schöllinen, on the St. Gothard, and the Verlohren Joch, on the Splugen, the gorge was absolutely impassable, and it was necessary to blast a passage through the huge masses of rock which blocked up the way. The poverty-stricken Canton of Uri had succeeded, with extreme difficulty, in scraping together the means to complete her part of the St. Gothard route, when a storm (August 1834) burst on the summit of the pass, which, in a few hours, swept away one-third of the road constructed at so much labour and cost. Five years later, a similar tempest effected nearly equal injury. And few years pass without some portion of the road being destroyed. In many places avalanches sweep

* The section of road at Gondo, measuring less than two hundred yards, required for its completion the incessant labour of one hundred workmen for eighteen months. In many places the labourers had to carry on their operations suspended from above by ropes, until a lodgment had been effected.

over the roads with destructive force, and it becomes necessary to construct galleries which shall defend travellers, and shoot the mass of snow and débris into the gorge below.

BRIEG, ON THE SIMPLON.

Murray supplies the facts respecting the construction of this magnificent road: "The construction of a route over the Simplon was decided upon by Napoleon immediately after the battle of Marengo, while the recollection of his own difficult passage of the Alps by the Great St. Bernard (at that time one of the easiest Alpine passes) was fresh in his memory. The plans and surveys by which the direction of the road was determined, were made by M. Céard, and a large portion of the works was executed under the superintendence of that able engineer. It was commenced on the Italian side in 1800, and on the Swiss in 1801. It took six years to complete, though it was barely passable in 1805, and more than thirty thousand men were employed on it at one time. To give a notion of the colossal nature of the undertaking, it may be mentioned that the number of bridges, great and small, constructed for the passage of the road between Brieg and Sesto, amounts to six hundred and eleven, in addition to the far more vast and costly constructions, such as terraces of massive masonry miles in length; of ten galleries, either cut out

Crossing an Alpine Pass in Winter.

of the living rock or built of solid stone; and of twenty houses of refuge to shelter travellers, and lodge the labourers constantly employed in taking care of the road. Its breadth is throughout at least twenty-five feet, in some places thirty feet, and the average slope nowhere exceeds six inches in six feet and a half.

"To use the eloquent words of Sir James Mackintosh, 'The Simplon may be safely said to be the most wonderful of useful works, because our canals and docks surpass it in utility, science, and magnitude, but they have no grandeur to the eye. Its peculiar character is, to be the greatest of all those monuments that at once dazzle the imagination by their splendour, and are subservient to general convenience.' The cost of this road averaged about 16,000*l.* per league. The object of Napoleon in its formation is well marked by the question which, on two different occasions, he first asked of the engineer sent to him to report progress—'*Le canon quand pourra-t-il passer au Simplon?*'"

Murray has given us the prose of the Simplon, Rogers shall supply us with its poetry:—

"Now the scene is changed;
And o'er the Simplon, o'er the Splugen winds
A path of pleasure. Like a silver zone
Flung about carelessly, it shines afar,
Catching the eye in many a broken link
In many a turn and traverse as it glides;
And oft above and oft below appears,
Seen o'er the wall by him who journeys up,
As if it were another, through the wild
Leading along he knows not whence or whither.
Yet through its fairy course, go where it will,
The torrent stops it not, the rugged rock
Opens and lets it in, and on it runs,
Winning its easy way from clime to clime
Through glens locked up before. . . .
But now 'tis passed
That turbulent Chaos; and the promised land
Lies at my feet in all its loveliness!
To him who starts up from a terrible dream,
And lo, the sun is shining, and the lark
Singing aloud for joy, to him is not
Such sudden ravishment as now I feel
At the first glimpses of fair Italy."

The passage of these roads in winter is attended with considerable danger from the accumulation of snow, and the violence of the tempests which burst upon the unwary traveller with appalling suddenness. The *Leisure Hour* for 1852 contains the narrative of "A Lady's Winter Adventure on the Simplon," which may serve to illustrate this, and to show the value of the refuges constructed at the most perilous points of the route. After describing the earlier portion of her journey, she says:—

"The darkness was increasing upon us every instant, and the snow on the road had now become so deep as to hide nearly half the wheels of the carriage, and cause the greatest difficulty in their turning at all. The snow being also newly fallen, was wholly untracked; and no wall or parapet being possible in this part of the road, the path is only divided from the edge of the precipice by occasional large, heavy, single stones. Against these we more than once heard the wheels of the carriage grate, proving how fearfully near the edge we were: and there really seemed nothing to guide or save our struggling horses from overstepping the almost imperceptible boundary that lay between us and

AVALANCHE GALLERY ON THE SIMPLON.

total destruction. It was a fearful scene, and one calculated to try the strongest nerves. The danger of our position really seemed frightful. Men and horses were blinded and driven back by the wind and incessant fall of snow which came direct against them; and though striving hard to get on, they constantly stumbled and fell in the untracked and deep snow. The horses could only by the greatest exertions be induced to face the gale, or move a step onwards, their labour being of course doubled by the difficulty of forcing the clogged wheels to advance at all. Night, and that too a fearful one of storm, was evidently fast approaching. What was to be done? I felt almost in despair, for it seemed to me absolutely impossible that we should this night pass beyond the place where we now were. But at this moment we stopped, and, hearing strange voices, I perceived that two men from the refuge had joined us: wild figures they were, enveloped in goat-skins, yet I hailed their arrival with joy and gratitude, for I felt sure that help was near. One soon advanced to me, and, announcing himself as the inspector of the Simplon road, and therefore, of course, the chief of the band of men thereon employed, assured me that, though our situation was certainly alarming, he hoped to be able to get us

ARRIVAL AT THE HOSPICE ON THE SIMPLON.

on to the Hospice. At last we arrived in front of a large and solid edifice, and stopping opposite to it, the inspector advised us to get out and proceed as well as we could on foot, for that it would be both a tedious and difficult operation in so deep a snow to turn the carriage, and get it into the *remise* or coach-house of the Hospice. We of course obeyed, as we should have done any directions he gave, and scrambling with great difficulty through the great masses of snow which covered the ground between us and the gate, chilled through and through, we at last arrived at the entrance, just as the great bell rang, and a monk, with three large dogs, came out to welcome and receive us.

"On entering the Hospice from the storm without, nothing could exceed the kindness of our reception. The refectory was warmed by an enormous stove, and seemed to us poor shivering wretches the very perfection of comfort; and the sight of it, joined to the hospitable welcome we received, was most cheering to those who, an hour before, had hardly known where they should pass the night. The monks assured us that their supper would be ready in less than an hour, but they were very anxious that we should immediately have some refreshment; we, however, declined this offer, and begged to wait for

A WINTER ADVENTURE ON THE SIMPLON.

the usual supper-time, for we had been too much alarmed and excited to feel very hungry. They then occupied themselves in seeing that rooms were immediately prepared for us, and the stoves lighted, so that they should be warm and comfortable by our bed-time. The *tourmente* now raging was, they said, a terrific one; and they added that we might indeed congratulate ourselves on being safely housed before night came on. In fact, as I afterwards accidentally ascertained, on this very day, on the Grand St. Bernard, where the *tourmente* was probably still more fearful, the clavandier of that Hospice, together with three servants and some dogs, were buried beneath an enormous avalanche from the Mont Mort, which covered them to the depth of fifteen feet, and of course all perished.

"We passed the time till supper in agreeable conversation with our kind and courteous hosts, profiting as much as possible from the delightful warmth of the great stove, and proceeded the next day across the pass in sledges, accompanied by a numerous body of guides."

Descending from the mountain on the southern side, the change is almost magical. A very few hours' ride, and all trace of winter is gone. Barren peaks, plains of ice and snow, roaring torrents, and storm-swept ravines have all been left behind. ITALY, with her fatal dower of beauty and fertility, has been reached.

"O Italy, how beautiful thou art!
Yet I could weep—for thou art lying, alas,
Low in the dust; and we admire thee now
As we admire the beautiful in death.
Thine was a dangerous gift, when thou wert born,
The gift of beauty. Would thou hadst it not;
Or wert as once awing the caitiff's vile
That now beset thee, making thee their slave!
Would they had loved thee less, or feared thee more!
But why despair? Twice hast thou lived already;
Twice shone among the nations of the world,
As the sun shines among the lesser lights
Of heaven; and shalt again. The hour shall come
When they who think to bind the ethereal spirit,
Who, like the eagle cowering o'er his prey,
Watch with quick eye, and strike and strike again
If but a sinew vibrate, shall confess
Their wisdom folly. Even now the flame
Bursts forth where once it burnt so gloriously,
And dying left a splendour like the day,
That like the day diffused itself and still
Blesses the earth."*

There is little difference between one small Italian town and another. They are all alike,—dirty, picturesque, glowing with colour, reeking with evil odours, thronged with an indolent, gossiping, excitable population eager to take part in every bargain, or to give advice about every piece of work which is going forward. Domo d'Ossola may serve for fifty others, each of which has the same narrow colonnaded streets, and littered pavements, and Lombardic architecture, and shops filled with fruit and sausages, maccaroni and garlic; bits of colour and light and shade which fill an artist with rapture; and poverty, dirt, and dilapidation, which inspire a comfortable cleanly English *paterfamilias* with disgust.

* Rogers' *Italy*.

DOMO D'OSSOLA.

Lady Morgan's description of Como is a photograph. "The interior of the town of Como," she says, "exhibits dark, narrow, and filthy streets; churches, numerous, old and tawdry; some gloomy palaces of the Comasque nobles, and dismantled dwellings of the *Cittadini*. The Duomo, founded in 1396, and constructed with marble from the neighbouring quarries, is its great feature. It stands happily with respect to the lake, but is surrounded with a small square of low, mouldering arcades and paltry little shops. Its baptistry is ascribed to Bramante; but the architecture is so mixed and semi-barbarous that it recalls the period when the arts began to revive in all the fantastic caprice of unsettled taste. Everywhere the elegant Gothic is mingled with the grotesque forms of ruder orders; and baṣo-relievos of monsters and nondescripts disfigure a façade, where light Gothic pinnacles are surmounted with golden crosses; while the fine-pointed arch and clustering columns contrast with staring saints and grinning griffins. . . . The interior of this ancient edifice has all the venerable character of the remote ages in which it rose and was completed. But its spacious nave, Gothic arches, and lofty dome, its masses of dark marbles and deep-tinted frescoes, are contrasted with such offerings from the

PALLANZA, LAGO MAGGIORE.

piety and gratitude of the Comasques, and the inhabitants of the neighbouring mountains, as would better suit the stalls of the Rue de Friperie, or the ware-rooms of Monmouth Street."

We may dismiss the Swiss-Italian lakes with almost equal brevity of description; for a very different reason, however, to that which prompts brevity in our notice of the towns. The stock of adjectives and exclamations on hand is finite, and soon exhausted. The first bend of the lake we come to will absorb them all. Every beat of the paddles, every stroke of the oar, will bring up some new combination of beauty, but a repetition of the stock phrases of admiration could only weary the reader:

"So I sit still,
And let the boatman shift his little sail,
His sail so forkèd and so swallow-like,
Well pleased with all that comes. The morning air
Plays on my cheek how gently, flinging round
A silvery gleam. And now the purple mists
Rise like a curtain; now the sun looks out,
Filling, o'erflowing with his glorious light,

This noble amphitheatre of hills;
And now appears as on a phosphorous sea
Numberless barks, from Milan, from Pavia,
Some sailing up, some down, and some at rest,
Lading, unlading, at that small town
Under the promontory—its tall tower
And long flat roofs, just such as Gaspar drew,
Caught by a sunbeam slanting through a cloud;
A quay-like scene, glittering and full of life,
And doubled by reflection."*

BOATS ON LAGO MAGGIORE.

Of the four principal lakes—Como, Lugano, Maggiore, and Orta—Orta is the smallest, but not the least beautiful. Each lake has its peculiar and distinctive charm, and so much depends upon atmospheric effects, upon the passing shades of feeling in the tourist's mind, and innumerable other circumstances which make up the sum-total of enjoyment, that it is difficult to express a preference which may be reversed at the next visit.

I saw the Lago d'Orta for the first time under exceptionally favourable circumstances. We left Omegna late in the afternoon, and when about half way across the lake, the sun went down in such a blaze of glory as I have never seen before or since. The whole atmosphere seemed flooded, saturated with golden light. The mountains which enclose the lake passed through all shades of colour from blue to deep rich purple. It was a fête day at some village on the banks, and the songs of revellers came faintly borne on the breeze, or, mingled with merry laughter, rang out from the boats on the lake. We told our rowers

* Rogers' *Italy*—"Como."

to slacken their speed, and, lying back on the cushioned seats, listened to those sweet sounds, gazed on those lovely scenes, and were lulled into the *dolce far niente*, so strange to the English, so dear to the Italian mind, by the rhythmic beat and tinkling drip of the oars as they softly rose and fell. Then came the night—and such a night! The sky was crystalline in its clearness, and thick sown with stars. The Milky Way, which looks so dim and blurred when seen through our misty air, was lustrous with light. The crescent moon was mirrored in the blue waters of the lake with wonderful vividness.

LUGANO.

In nothing do judgments vary more than respecting the Borromean Islands in Lago Maggiore. Hazlitt sneers at the Isola Bella as "a piece of confectionery hung about with wreaths of flowers," and Matthews glorifies it as "the magic creation of labour and taste—a fairy land, which might serve as a model for the gardens of Calypso." De Saussure thought it "a magnificent caprice, a sublime conception, a sort of creation;" to Simond it suggested "a Perigord pie stuck round with heads of game." Most visitors will assent to the truth of Murray's criticism: "To taste it may have little pretension; but to a traveller fresh from the rigid climate of the north this singular creation of art, with its aromatic groves, its aloes and cactuses starting out of the rocks,

ISOLA BELLA, LAGO MAGGIORE.

and, above all, its glorious situation, bathed by the dark blue waters of the lake, reflecting the sparkling white villages on its banks, and the distant snows of the Alps, cannot fail to afford pleasure." Even the most cynical and censorious will admit that the views from the terraces combine everything which can be imagined as the perfection of a romantic and luxurious abode. The deep clear blue water laps gently round the rocks. Vistas of distant sunny hills and valleys open out from beneath the shade of bowers of roses, through gaps in the olive and the cactus. Purple mountains and snow-peaks glimmer from afar through the flickering leaves and blossoms of an orange-grove. It may be a mere piece of confectionery, in execrable taste, but there is no denying that it is a lovely spot.

Let no person claim to know the Italian lakes fully till he has seen them lashed to fury in tempest. When seen, it is a sight never to be forgotten. Once at the close of a sultry day, I saw a pile of angry clouds grow up with a weird and terrible rapidity over the mountain-tops. Down each valley which debouched upon the lake vast masses of vapour came pouring, like the armies of ghosts in Ossian, no sooner reaching the open space than the wind dissipated them. The sky waxed darker and darker. The soft, blue lake, which, through the day had been smooth as oil and scarcely furrowed by a ripple, began to toss restlessly, and the waves, rolling shoreward, broke in foam upon the terraced gardens. Then came a single flash, followed by a peal of thunder, which echoed and reverberated amongst the hills as though it would never cease. It was like the cannon which gives the signal for a general engagement. Instantly, a deluge of rain poured down, flash succeeded to flash, peal to peal, without intermission, till, shortly before midnight, the storm rolled away, the full moon shone out in undimmed radiance, and the lake seemed to roll in a flood of living silver. But all night long we could hear the distant thunder bellowing in the direction of Monte Rosa, and the horizon was lit up every few seconds by soft sheet-lightning. It was impossible not to think of that memorable night, eighteen centuries ago, when the Galilean lake was lashed to fury by such a storm, and the Divine voice was heard, saying, "Peace: be still; and the wind ceased, and there was a great calm."

STORM ON LAKE COMO.

Venice is now so easily accessible that a large proportion of those who visit the lakes extend their journey so as to reach this glorious old city, the picturesque beauty of which has been illustrated by both poet and painter.

"There is a glorious city in the sea.
The sea is in the broad, the narrow streets,
Ebbing and flowing; and the salt sea-weed
Clings to the marble of her palaces.
No track of men, no footsteps to and fro,
Lead to her gates. The path lies o'er the sea
Invisible; and from the land we went,
As to a floating city—steering in,
And gliding up her streets as in a dream,
So smoothly, silently—by many a dome,
Mosque-like, and many a stately portico,

The statues ranged along an azure sky;
By many a pile in more than eastern pride,
Of old the residence of merchant kings;
The fronts of some, though time had shattered them,
Still glowing with the richer hues of art,
As though the wealth within them had run o'er."*

The approach to Venice from the mainland is very striking, and the general aspect of the city is exceedingly picturesque. Mr. Ruskin describes both, with his usual eloquence, in his *Stones of Venice:*

"As the boat drew nearer to the city, the coast which the traveller had just left sank behind him into one long, low, sad-coloured line, tufted irregularly with brushwood and willows; but, at what seemed its northern extremity, the hills of Arqua rose in a dark cluster of purple pyramids, balanced on the bright mirage of the lagoon; two or three smooth surges of inferior hill extended themselves about their roots, and beyond these, beginning with the craggy peaks above Vicenza, the chain of the Alps girded the whole horizon to the north—a wall of jagged blue, here and there showing through its clefts a wilderness of misty precipices, fading far back into the recesses of Cadore, and itself rising and breaking away eastward, where the sun struck opposite upon its snow, into mighty fragments of peaked light, standing up behind the barred clouds of evening, one after another, countless, the crown of the Adrian Sea, until the eye turned back from pursuing them, to rest upon the nearer burning of the campaniles of Murano, and on the great city, where it magnified itself along the waves, as the quick silent pacing of the gondola drew nearer and nearer. And at last, when its walls were reached, and the outmost of its untrodden streets was entered, not through towered gate or guarded rampart, but as a deep inlet between two rocks of coral in the Indian Sea; when first upon the traveller's sight opened the long ranges of columned palaces—each with its black boat moored at the portal; each with its image cast down beneath its feet, upon that green pavement which every breeze broke into new fantasies of rich tesselation; when first, at the extremity of the bright vista, the shadowy Rialto threw its colossal curve slowly forth from behind the palace of the Camerlenghi; that strange curve, so delicate, so adamantine, strong as a mountain cavern, graceful as a bow just bent; when first, before its moonlike circumference was all risen, the gondolier's cry, 'Ah! Stali,' struck sharp upon the ear, and the prow turned aside under the mighty cornices that half met over the narrow canal, where the plash of the water followed close and loud, ringing along the marble by the boat's side; and when at last that boat darted forth upon the breadth of silver sea, across which the front of the Ducal palace, flushed with its sanguine veins, looks to the snowy dome of Our Lady of Salvation, it was no marvel that the mind should be so deeply entranced by the visionary charm of a scene so beautiful and so strange, as to forget the darker truths of its history and its being. . . .

* Rogers' *Italy*—Venice.

THE BRIDGE OF SIGHS.

BRONZE HORSES OF ST. MARK.

"Between those pillars there opens a great light, and, in the midst of it, as we advance slowly, the vast tower of St. Mark seems to lift itself visibly forth from the level field of chequered stones; and on each side, the countless arches prolong themselves into ranged symmetry, as if the rugged and irregular houses that pressed together above us in the dark alley had been struck back into sudden obedience and lovely order, and all their rude casements and broken walls had been transformed into arches charged with goodly sculpture, and fluted shafts of delicate stone.

"And well may they fall back, for beyond those troops of ordered arches there rises a vision out of the earth, and all the great square seems to have opened from it in a kind of awe, that we may see it far away;—a multitude of pillars and white domes, clustered into a long low pyramid of coloured light, a treasure-heap, it seems, partly of gold, and partly of opal and mother-of-pearl, hollowed beneath into five great vaulted porches, ceiled with fair mosaic, and beset with sculpture of alabaster, clear as amber and delicate as ivory,—sculpture; fantastic and involved, of palm leaves and lilies, and grapes and pomegranates, and birds clinging and fluttering among the branches, all twined together into an endless network of buds and plumes; and, in the midst of it, the solemn forms of angels, sceptred, and robed to the feet, and leaning to each other across the gates, their figures indistinct among the gleaming of the golden ground through the leaves beside them, interrupted and dim, like the morning light as it faded back among the branches of Eden, when first its gates were angel-guarded long ago. And round the walls of the porches there are set pillars of variegated stones, jasper and porphyry, and deep green serpentine spotted with flakes of snow, and marbles, that half refuse and half yield to the sunshine, Cleopatra-like, 'their bluest veins to kiss,'—the shadow, as it steals back from them, revealing line after line of azure undulation, as a receding tide leaves the waved sand; their capitals rich with interwoven tracery, rooted knots of herbage, and drifting leaves of acanthus and vine, and mystical signs, all beginning and ending in the Cross; and above them, in the broad archivolts, a continuous change of language and of life—angels, and the signs of heaven and the labours of men, each in its appointed season upon the earth; and above these another range of glittering pinnacles, mixed with white arches edged with scarlet flowers,—a confusion of delight, amidst which the breasts of the Greek horses are seen blazing in their breadth of golden strength, and the St. Mark's Lion, lifted on a blue field covered with stars, until at last, as if in ecstasy, the crests of the arches break into a marble foam, and toss themselves far into the blue sky in flashes and wreaths of sculptured spray, as if the breakers on the Lido shore had been frost-bound before they fell, and the sea-nymphs had inlaid them with coral and amethyst."

Venice of to-day affords a melancholy combination of the traces of ancient wealth and grandeur, with the indications of modern poverty and decay; though, like its ancient rivals, it is beginning to share in the commercial revival and political activity of the new Italian kingdom.

"Once did she hold the gorgeous east in fee;
And was the safeguard of the west: the worth
Of Venice did not fall below her birth,
Venice, the oldest child of Liberty!
She was a maiden city, bright and free;
No guile seduced, no force could violate;
And, when she took unto herself a mate,
She must espouse the everlasting sea.
And what if she has seen those glories fade,
Those titles vanish, and that strength decay;
Yet shall some tribute of respect be paid
When her long life hath reached its final day;
Men are we, and must grieve when even the shade
Of that which once was great is passed away."

THE MONTE ROSA DISTRICT.

'TWIXT LIFE AND DEATH.

THE MONTE ROSA DISTRICT.

THE VAL ANZASCA—MACUGNAGA—HEAD OF THE VAL ANZASCA—PASS OF MONTE MORO—SAAS—THE WEISSTHOR—ZERMATT—GLACIERS—THE MATTERHORN—ASCENT OF THE MATTERHORN.

BROCKEDON, describing the Val Anzasca and the pass of the Monte Moro, says, "My recollections of the scenes through which I have passed in the last three days from Visp to Vogogna, induce me to think this pass the most wild, interesting, and beautiful that I have yet made, and the Val Anzasca I have distinguished in my mind as the Happy Valley." Most tourists will concur in the estimate expressed by so competent a judge. It would be difficult to imagine anything more grandly imposing than the pass, or more exquisitely beautiful than the valley. Every element of sublimity and beauty are combined, each in the highest perfection. The foliage and vegetation are Italian in richness and profusion. The vines, unlike those of France and Germany, are trained in wild luxuriance along

MACUGNAGA CHURCH.

trellised *berceaux*, or hang in festoons from tree to tree. The gloomy pine woods have given place to mighty forests of chestnut and beech, which clothe the mountain sides in robes of richest verdure. The glades beneath these giant trees are gay with innumerable flowers. Smooth slopes, grassy knolls, and dells of brightest green allure the eye or invite the traveller to rest in the refreshing shade. Right across the valley, dominating the whole landscape, with edges clear cut against the sky, stretch the white snows of Monte Rosa.

It is not till near Borca that the valley loses its Italian character and becomes Alpine in its savage sublimity. Even at Macugnaga, immediately at the foot of Monte Rosa, there is an exuberant fertility and a richness of colour perceptibly unlike the sterility of villages situated at a similar elevation on the northern side of the chain.

SAAS.

Macugnaga is set in the midst of some wonderful scenery. The village looks as if it were at the bottom of everything, as all the views from it may be said to be upward; but in reality it is about five thousand feet above the level of the sea; i.e., much above the top of Snowdon. The church with its noble linden tree, said to be three hundred years old, forms a striking object in the landscape. Here, as everywhere on the south side of the Alps, shrines and bone-houses strike the eye at every turn. The latter are, to the eye of an Englishman, repulsive objects. If they inspired reverential thoughts of another life, or seemed to express tender loving memories of the departed, it would be possible to become reconciled to them. But no such feelings are discernible.

Skulls and bones are covered with mould and dirt—the accumulation of years of neglect.

The chief points in the magnificent view from the head of the Val Anzasca are well sketched in King's *Italian Valleys of the Alps*: "After the heavy rain, every rivulet was pouring down the mountain sides; and a fine waterfall above Vanzone was a broad sheet of foaming cascades from the summit of the cliff, over which it fell in thundering volume. The narrow lanes traversed a complete forest of noble overshadowing chestnuts and walnuts, glowing with the orange tints of autumn. Bright green mosses and luxuriant ferns in the richest profusion carpeted the stone walls and rocky nooks, shaded by the spreading trees. . . . When the sun rose next morning, Monte Rosa unveiled, and presented a truly magnificent and startling spectacle, as we left the little inn for the Macugnaga Glacier, and advanced up the valley. The panorama, in its colossal magnitude, was superb, when we got an unobstructed view from the open basin in which lie the scattered hamlets of Macugnaga. This view of Monte Rosa can only be compared in grandeur to that of its rival, Mont Blanc, from the Val d'Entrèves; though in our estimation it is much the more imposing of the two. After the late storm it was sheeted, from its highest pinnacle to the lower glacier, with sparkling snow; hardly a projecting crag was uncovered until the sun began to exercise its power; while the enormous face of the mountain was a perfectly inaccessible precipice, some ten thousand feet in height, and of awful steepness. The view of the summits from here commenced with the Signal Kuppe; the other peaks seen from the Pile Alpe being hidden behind its retreating angle. Next were the Zumstein Spitze; the Höchste Spitze, with its double points; and now, at a considerable interval, the Nord End, which from the Combetta had seemed but a protuberance of the Höchste Spitze. To the left of Monte Rosa the smooth snowy cone of the Pizzo Bianco appeared above a forest-covered crest; an exquisite object in itself, and also associated with Saussure's ascent of it, to compare the heights of the peaks of Monte Rosa. All this, however, was but a portion of the stupendous curtain of snow-clad mountains which stretched right across the outspreading head of the valley. From the Nord End, a long and lower, but only less magnificent crest, extended in serried wildness up to the advanced guards of the Monte Moro. In the centre of them was the Weissthor, over which is a perilous and rarely-effected pass into the Saas Thal; and farther to the right, the crags of the Cima di Jazi."

From Macugnaga the pass over the Monte Moro to Saas is one of the grandest in Switzerland. A steep ascent for about a couple of hours, partly through pine forest, partly over the bare mountain-side, brings the tourist to the edge of the snow. The views in the ascent are magnificent. The Cima di Jazi and the precipices of Monte Rosa are full in view the whole way, and are of inconceivable grandeur. Their huge masses are the more imposing from there striking contrast with the rich luxuriant foliage of the valley at their base.

About an hour, or an hour and a half, over the snow brings the tourist to the summit of the pass, from which he looks down into the vast concave formed by the flanks of Monte Rosa. Mr. Ball, no mean authority on all questions connected with Alpine scenery, says of the view from this point:

HEAD OF THE VAL ANZASCA.

"Many of the passes described in this section may tempt more strongly the adventurous traveller, who loves the flavour of difficulty, not to say danger; but there is, perhaps, none which offers a scene of such surpassing grandeur as that here unrolled before his eyes; and certainly none which deserve a preference.

EAGLE AND CHAMOIS.

The eastern face of Monte Rosa, with the continuous range of precipice that extends to the Weissthor, is here seen from the most favourable point of view, and the beautiful peak of the Pizzo Bianco, on the opposite side of the basin of Macugnaga, completes the wonderful picture."

A little over the summit of the pass, on the northern side, the vestiges of a paved road are reached, which seems strangely out of place here. Once, however, this route, now used only by smugglers and tourists, was much frequented, and formed the highway between the Vallais and the Val Anzasca. Tradition connects the road with the Moors, whose traces are to be found on both sides the pass, and from whom its name is said to have been derived.* There is no very clear historical account as to how the Moors penetrated to, or why they settled in, such a remote out-of-the-way district; but the fact seems tolerably well attested.

Macugnaga and the neighbourhood are especially interesting to the naturalist. The valleys are rich in rare and beautiful flowers. The whistle of the marmot may be heard in every glen. The lammergeier and golden eagle may be descried, poised high up in the clear blue sky, or wheeling slowly round some solitary peak; and herds of chamois may be seen in the early morning on the heights overlooking the ordinary route of tourists. In most parts of Switzerland this wild denizen of the mountains has become very rare. From many districts it has disappeared altogether, except in almost inaccessible recesses where the hunter cannot follow, and where, of course, the passing visitor has no chance of getting a sight of it. But I have seldom crossed any of the passes in this district without seeing several.

The ordinary pedestrian desirous of proceeding to Zermatt, or the Rhone Valley, will continue his journey northward through the village of Saas, along a wild glen to Stalden, at which place the two branches of the valley unite. The more adventurous mountaineer will probably attempt the passage of the Weissthor. This pass presents no very serious difficulty to expert climbers, but it is a severe pull for those who are not in training; and at one or two points is trying to persons who cannot creep along the edge of a precipice without giddiness. A recent number of the *Leisure Hour* describes the passage of the Weissthor:

"We rose at three, dressed by candle-light, with a very uncomfortable sort of feeling that we wished the work done, and Zermatt safely reached. We got away at five minutes to four, and walked up the valley for nearly an hour, calling at a *châlet* for the rope, etc., Lochmatter overtaking us with his ice-axe. We enjoyed the sight of the sun tipping the ridges of Monte Rosa and the other mountains, as it came upon us, and the transition from darkness to dawn was very striking. We soon began to ascend by a rough path, sometimes over rocks, and sometimes through water, till, in about another hour, we reached a poor *châlet*.

* The names of many of the peaks north of Monte Rosa have clearly a Moorish origin, *e. g.*, Mischabel, Almagel, Alphubel, Allalein. The villages of Allmengal, Aballa, and Balen have probably a similar derivation.

"From this point the ascent began in earnest, and an hour's toiling over rocks and precipitous ledges tried us very severely. We could not help resting every now and then, and our guides became a little impatient, assuring us that, '*Comme ça nous n'arriverons jamais.*' It was no use talking, it was tremendous work. The cliff was nearly perpendicular, each step being a separate climb. The higher we went, the more fearful seemed the precipice we were scaling on

HEAD OF CHAMOIS.

looking below. After another sharp tug, the guides advised a glass of wine and a crust. This we had, and then got on better, the guides soon telling us we had walked well the last hour. We now approached a difficulty, consisting of a steep slope of snow, like the roof of a Gothic church. The rope was now called into requisition, and we were all attached to it. Lochmatter cut some steps with his axe, and started up. T—— then put his feet into the holes, and followed him, I next, and the other guide last. We stood still while fresh steps were cut, when the process was repeated; and in this way, after much slipping and tumbling, we gained the top of the slope, and took to the rocks again. Hence to the summit was really difficult and dangerous, being a zigzag climb up the face of the rock, with a foot-hold of from six to twelve inches wide, and, as Murray descibes it, 'hanging on by the eyelids.'

ON THE WEISSTHOR.

"Soon we came to the 'Cheminée,' a narrow space between two rocks, so smooth and perpendicular as to suggest the idea that only a sweep could get up. Lochmatter went up like a cat, and the other guide, placing me in a delightful ledge about twelve inches square, made T—— stand on his shoulders like an acrobat, and shot him up to Lochmatter, who dexterously caught him and dragged him up. I was shot up in the same way, and the guide came scrambling after anyhow. We looked at each other in astonishment at what we had done. '*Encore une demi-heure*,' said Lochmatter, '*et nous arriverons au sommet.*' Then it was '*vingt*,' and then '*dix minutes*;' and finally, not before we wanted it, '*le sommet*' was announced.

"It was a clear space about ten feet by five feet, at the end of a ridge of

ROPED TOGETHER ON A SNOW SLOPE.

rock, and apparently the only point at which the ridge could be turned at all. Here, carefully arranging our legs so as not to kick each other over, we prepared to dine. It was twelve exactly, the sun was burning us, and there was not a vestige of shade. Looking the way we had come, beyond the distant peaks, we saw a lake, which our guide declared was Lago Maggiore.

"On the other side, the way we had yet to go, appeared boundless fields of *neve*, or snow, with a few black rocks cropping up here and there, the Matterhorn and other well-known peaks towering above them. It was a wonderful sight, but so hot that, after we had eaten all we could, we soon crept amongst some rocks in hopes of a little shelter. This we did not find; but it blew fresher on this side, and we were obliged to be content with that. After awhile we prepared to descend this interminable plateau of snow; the heat of the sun had of course made it very soft, and we sank up to our knees at every step. We tried a glissade, but it was impossible;* so we were forced to push on as best we could. We passed close under the tremendous Cima di Jazi, whose

TRYING A GLISSADE.

overhanging cornice seemed as if it would fall and crush us, skirting several yawning crevasses, and we were four weary hours before we got off the snow on to the solid ice of the Gorner glacier. This was harder to the feet, but sloppy and uncomfortable. Presently we reached the first rock of the lateral moraine, and under its shelter we all lay down and slept for about three quarters of an hour. We passed quite round the base of Monte Rosa, and, sometimes on rocks, sometimes on the glacier, we at length struck into the path leading to the

* The glissade is effected by thrusting the heels firmly in the snow, throwing the head well back, and steadying the body with the alpenstock, which serves as a support, a drag, and a balancing-pole. A slope of snow may thus be glided down rapidly and pleasantly, with the danger, however, to the inexperienced, of toppling forward, and thus coming to grief.

MONTE ROSA FROM THE GORNER-GRAT.

Riffel Hotel. Hence a short and easy walk brought us to Zermatt, one of the noblest centres of grand scenery in the world."

There is no place in Switzerland which has risen so rapidly in public favour as Zermatt, or "Young Chamouni," as it is sometimes called. Its situation is surpassingly fine, lying, as it does, in a great natural basin, into which six glaciers fall. There is a great and charming variety of scenery—savage and grand, as well as peaceful and tender. The torrents as they emerge from the glacier-caves are turbid and impetuous, roaring amongst the boulders of the moraines or plunging in cataracts down the rocks. But gradually they subside into a comparative calm, and may be found flowing peacefully through the rich green meadows from which Zermatt takes its name.* Leaving the valley, and climbing the Gorner-grat, or the Hörnli, we stand face to face with some of the grandest mountains in Europe:—Monte Rosa, the Lyskamm, the Breithorn, the tremendous Matterhorn with its ten thousand feet of precipice, and a host of others—monuments of the Creator's power, to us objects of awe and wonder. The glaciers which debouche upon the valley—the Gorner, the Theodule, the Furgge, the Zmutt, and the Trift—all possess points of interest. The first of these, one of the longest in Switzerland, is steadily advancing, ploughing up the ground before it, and demolishing villages in its destructive course.

* Zermatt is connected in etymology with the German *Matt*, a meadow; meaning either "upon the meadow," or, as some suppose, "the destroyed meadow," like Champéry. Similarly, the Matterhorn is "the horn or peak of the meadows."

These vast rivers of ice are so easily accessible from Zermatt, that they afford favourable opportunities for the study of glacial phenomena. Huge masses of moraine are heaped up by the glacier along its flanks, or at its termination. Fearful crevasses cleave its depths, down which one may look as into a fathomless abyss of green, or blue, or white crystal, and into which whoso falls finds a sepulchre of ice. Strange and seemingly contradictory effects are produced by rocks and stones on the surface of the ice-plain. Sometimes they sink into its mass, melting the ice upon which they rest through their absorption of solar heat; sometimes they rise high above the general mass upon pinnacles kept from melting by the shadow they cast. But more impressive than all is the steady continuous advance of the whole mass of the glacier as it creeps forward daily and hourly into the valley below. These and kindred phenomena may all be observed with the utmost facility at Zermatt.

GLACIER TABLE.

Professor J. D. Forbes, one of the highest scientific authorities upon these questions, has, in an eloquent passage, given some valuable suggestions on the moral teachings of the glaciers:—"Poets and philosophers have delighted to compare the course of human life to that of a river; perhaps a still apter simile might be found in the history of a glacier. Heaven-descended in its origin, it yet takes its mould and conformation from the hidden womb of the mountains which brought it forth. At first soft and ductile, it acquires a character and firmness of its own as an inevitable destiny urges it on its onward career. Jostled and constrained by the crosses and inequalities of its prescribed path, hedged in by impassable barriers which fix limits to its movements, it yields groaning to its fate, and still travels forward, seamed with the scars of many a conflict with opposing obstacles. All this while, although wasting, it is renewed by an unseen power; it evaporates, but is not consumed. On its surface it bears the spoils which, during the progess of existence, it had made its own—often weighty burdens devoid of beauty or value, at times precious masses, sparkling with gems or with ore. Having at length attained its greatest width and extension, commanding admiration by its beauty and power, waste predominates over supply, the vital springs begin to fail, it stoops into an attitude of decrepitude; it drops the burdens, one by one, which it had borne so proudly aloft: its dissolution is inevitable. But as it is resolved into its elements, it takes all at once a new and livelier, and disembarrassed form; from the wreck of its members it arises another, yet the same—a noble, full-bodied, arrowy stream, which leaps rejoicing over the obstacles which before had stayed its progress, and hastens through fertile valleys towards a freer existence, and a final union in the ocean with the boundless and the infinite."

CREVASSES.

But it is the Matterhorn which forms the distinctive and supreme glory of the Zermatt valley. Most mountains which rise above the line of perpetual snow possess a certain amount of similarity which permits, nay invites, comparison with one another. Mont Blanc, Monte Rosa, the Jungfrau, resemble each other in rising into a dome, more or less irregular, covered with ice and snow. The Matterhorn, as seen from Zermatt, stands alone and incomparable. Its northern face appears a single obelisk of rock rising, naked and precipitous, from the sea of *névé* and glacier about its base. "Other peaks," says Mr. Ball, "such as some of the Chamouni Aiguilles, may appear as bold in outline, but they want the air of solidity peculiar to this unmatched peak. With an audacity that seems to defy the universe, it rears its front five thousand feet above the snow-fields at its base, as though its massive framework could support the shock of a world in ruins." The author of the *Regular Swiss Round* grotesquely compares it to what, when a little boy, he fancied the North Pole must be at the end of the round world.

THE MORAINE.

MONTE ROSA FROM THE MONTE MORO.

The appearance of imperishable solidity which the Matterhorn presents is, however, delusive. Really it is crumbling away every day and every hour, though, from its immense mass, centuries, even millenniums must pass before the decay will be perceptible in its diminished bulk. Massive strength is the impression produced on every spectator by the mighty bastions of rock which compose the Matterhorn. Mr. Ruskin says of it, "Unlike the Chamouni Aiguilles, there is no aspect of destruction about the Matterhorn cliffs. They are not torn remnants of separating spires, yielding flake by flake, and band by band, to the continual process of decay. They are, on the contrary, an unaltered monument, seemingly sculptured long ago, the huge walls retaining yet the forms into which they were first engraved, and standing like an Egyptian temple,—delicate-fronted, softly-coloured, the suns of uncounted ages rising and falling upon it continually, but still casting the same line of shadows from east to west, still, century after century, touching the same purple stains on the Lotus pillars, while the desert-sand ebbs and flows about their feet, as those autumn leaves of rock lie heaped about the base of the Cervin."

ON THE MATTERHORN.

For many years the Matterhorn defied all attempts to scale its summit. It remained inaccessible, unconquerable. One after another of the mountaineers of the Alpine Club was repulsed from its overhanging and unconquerable sides. The year 1865 will be for ever memorable in the annals of Swiss mountaineering, from the terrible tragedy which followed upon the first successful attempt, in which Lord Francis Douglas, the Rev. Charles Hudson, Mr. Hadow, and Michel Croz, of Chamouni, perished. The following is Mr. Whymper's narrative, slightly abridged:—

"We left Zermatt at 5·35 on Thursday morning, taking the two young Taugwalders as porters. They carried provisions for the whole party for three days, in case the ascent should prove more difficult than we anticipated.

"On the first day we did not intend to ascend to any great height, but to stop when we found a good position for placing the tent. We mounted accordingly very leisurely, left the Lac Noir at 8·20, and passed along the ridge connecting the Hörnli with the actual peak, at the foot of which we arrived at 11·20, having frequently halted on the way. We then quitted the ridge, went to the left, and ascended by the north-eastern face of the mountain. Before 12 o'clock we had found a good position for the tent, at a height of 11,000 feet; but Croz and the elder of Taugwalder's sons went on to look what was above, in order to save time on the following morning. The remainder constructed the platform on which the tent was to be placed; and by the time this was finished, the two men returned, reported joyfully that as far as they had gone they had seen nothing but that which was good, and asserted positively that had we gone on with them on that day we could have ascended the mountain, and have returned to the tent with facility. We passed the remaining hours of daylight—some basking in the sunshine, some sketching or collecting, and, when the sun went down, giving, as it departed, a glorious promise for the morrow, we returned to the tent to arrange for the night. Hudson made tea, myself coffee, and we then retired, each one to his blanket bag; the Taugwalders, Lord Francis Douglas, and myself occupying the tent, the others remaining, by preference, outside. But long after dusk the cliffs above echoed with our laughter and with the songs of the guides, for we were happy that night in camp, and did not dream of calamity.

THE BLANKET BAG.*

"We were astir long before daybreak on the morning of the 14th, and started directly it was possible to move, leaving the youngest of Taugwalder's sons behind. At 6·20 we had attained a height of 12,800 feet, and halted for half an hour, then continued the ascent without a break until 9·55, when we stopped for fifty minutes, at a height probably of about 14,000 feet. Thus far we had ascended by the north-eastern face of the mountain, and had not met with a single difficulty. For the greater part of the way there was, indeed, no occasion for the rope; and sometimes Hudson led, sometimes myself. We had now arrived at the foot of that part which from Zermatt seems perpendicular or overhanging, and we could no longer continue on the same side. By common

* This illustration, and that on page 105, are from *Scrambles amongst the Alps*. By E. Whymper. A personal narrative, full of interest for Alpine tourists and for all lovers of adventure, with much new and valuable information.

consent, therefore, we ascended for some distance by the *arête*—that is, by the ridge descending towards Zermatt—and then turned over to the right, or to the north-western face. The general slope of the mountain at this part was less than 40°, and snow had consequently accumulated and filled up the irregularities

A CANNONADE ON THE MATTERHORN.

of the rock face, leaving only occasional fragments projecting here and there. These were at times coated with a thin glaze of ice, from the snow above having melted and frozen again during the night. Still it was a place over which any fair mountaineer might pass in safety. We found, however, that Mr. Hadow was not accustomed to this kind of work, and required assistance. It is only fair to say the difficulty experienced by Mr. Hadow at this part arose, not from fatigue or lack of courage, but simply and entirely from want of experience. Mr. Hudson, who followed me, passed over this part, and, as far as I know, ascended the entire mountain without having the slightest assistance rendered to him on any occasion. Sometimes, after I had taken a hand from Croz or received a pull, I turned to give the same to Hudson, but he invariably declined, saying it was not necessary. This solitary difficult path was of no great extent, certainly not more than 300 feet high, and after it was passed, the angles became less and less as we approached the summit; at last the slope was so moderate, that Croz and myself detached ourselves from the others, and ran on to the top. We arrived there at 1.40 p.m., the others about ten minutes after us.

"I have been requested to describe particularly the state of the party on the summit. No one showed any sign of fatigue, neither did I hear anything to lead me to suppose that any one was at all tired. I remember Croz laughing at me when I asked him the question. We had, indeed, been moving less than ten hours, and during that time had halted for nearly two. The only remark which I heard suggestive of danger was made by Croz, but it was quite casual, and probably meant nothing. He said, after I had remarked that we had come up very slowly, 'Yes; I would rather go down with you and another guide alone than with those who are going.' As to ourselves, we were arranging what we should do that night on our return to Zermatt.

SKETCH MAP OF THE ROUTE OF ASCENT.

"We remained on the summit for one hour, and during the time Hudson and I consulted, as we had done all the day, as to the best and safest arrangement of the party. We agreed that it would be best for Croz to go first, as he was the most powerful, and Hadow second; Hudson, who was equal to a guide in sureness of foot, wished to be third; Lord F. Douglas was placed next, and old Taugwalder, the strongest of the remainder, behind him. I suggested to Hudson that we should attach a rope to the rocks on our arrival at the difficult bit, and hold it as we descended, as an additional protection. He approved the idea, but it was not definitely settled that it should be done. The party was being arranged in the above order while I was making a sketch of the summit,

THE MATTERHORN.

and they were waiting for me to be tied in my place, when some one remembered that we had not left our names in a bottle; they requested me to write them, and moved off while it was being done. A few minutes afterwards I tied myself to young Taugwalder, and followed, catching them just as they were commencing the descent of the difficult part described above. The greatest care was being taken. Only one man was moving at a time; when he was firmly planted the next advanced, and so on. The average distance between each was probably twenty feet.

"I was, as I have explained, detached from the others, and following them; but after about a quarter of an hour Lord F. Douglas asked me to tie on to old Taugwalder, as he feared, he said, that if there was a slip, Taugwalder would not be able to hold him. This was done hardly ten minutes before the accident, and undoubtedly saved Taugwalder's life.

"As far as I know, at the moment of the accident, no one was actually moving. I cannot speak with certainty, neither can the Taugwalders, because the two leading men were partially hidden from our sight by an intervening mass of rock. Poor Croz had laid aside his axe, and, in order to give Mr. Hadow greater security, was absolutely taking hold of his legs and putting his feet, one by one, into their proper positions. From the movements of their shoulders it is my belief that Croz, having done as I have said, was in the act of turning round to go down a step or two himself; at this moment Mr. Hadow slipped, fell on him, and knocked him over. I heard one startled exclamation from Croz, then saw him and Mr. Hadow flying downwards; in another moment Hudson was dragged from his steps and Lord F. Douglas immediately after him. All this was the work of a moment; but immediately we heard Croz's exclamation, Taugwalder and myself planted ourselves as firmly as the rocks would permit; the rope was tight between us, and the shock came on us both as on one man. We held; but the rope broke midway between Taugwalder and Lord F. Douglas. For two or three seconds we saw our unfortunate companions sliding downwards on their backs, and spreading out their hands endeavouring to save themselves; they then disappeared one by one, and fell from precipice to precipice on to the Matterhorn glacier below, a distance of nearly four thousand feet in height. From the moment the rope broke it was impossible to help them.

"For the space of half an hour we remained on the spot without moving a single step. The two men, paralysed with terror, cried like infants, and trembled in such a manner as to threaten us with the fate of the others. Immediately we had ascended to a safe place, I asked for the rope that had broken, and to my surprise—indeed, to my horror—found that it was the weakest of the three ropes. As the first five men had been tied while I was sketching, I had not noticed the rope they employed; and now I could only conclude that they had seen fit to use this in preference to the others. It has been stated that the rope broke in consequence of its fraying over a rock; this is not the case, it broke in mid-air, and the end does not show any trace of previous injury.

"For more than two hours afterwards I thought every moment that the next would be my last; for the Taugwalders, utterly unnerved, were not only incapable of giving assistance, but were in such a state that a slip might have been expected from one or the other at any moment. I do the younger man, moreover, no injustice when I say that, immediately we got to the easy part of the descent, he was able to laugh, smoke, and eat as if nothing had happened. There is no occasion to say more of the descent. I looked frequently, but in vain, for traces of my unfortunate companions, and we were in consequence surprised by the night when still at a height of 13,000 feet. We arrived at Zermatt at 10·30 on Saturday morning.

"Immediately on my arrival I sent to the President of the Commune, and requested him to send as many men as possible to ascend heights whence the spot could be commanded where I knew the four must have fallen. A number went, and returned after six hours, reporting they had seen them, but that they could not reach them that day. They proposed starting on Sunday evening, so as to reach the bodies at daybreak on Monday; but, unwilling to lose the slightest chance, the Rev. J. McCormick and myself resolved to start on Sunday morning. By 8·30 we had got on to the plateau, and within sight of the corner in which we knew my companions must be. As we saw one weather-beaten man after another raise the telescope, turn deadly pale, and pass it on without a word to the next, we knew that all hope was gone. We approached; they had fallen below as they had fallen above—Croz a little in advance, Hadow near him, and Hudson some distance behind; but of Lord F. Douglas we could see nothing."

This affecting narrative may be supplemented by a few extracts from that of the Rev. J. McCormick, Mr. Hudson's companion and intimate friend. Describing an early period of their tour, he says:

"Later in the day Hudson came into my room to join me in prayer before ascending Mont Blanc. How earnestly, simply, and cheerfully he told his own and his friend's wants to God! In all humility, yet with holy boldness, he spake to the Lord of heaven and earth, 'as a man talketh to his friend'—as a child to his father. I could not, and would not if I could, make known all that he said. Yet I think I ought to state that he used words to this effect with reference to our contemplated excursion:—'Heavenly Father, we remember Thee in the midst of our work, and trials: let us not forget Thee in our pleasures. Thou hast made these glorious mountains and this splendid scenery for our happiness; while enjoying them, give to us bright thoughts of Thyself. Our strength of body is from Thee; be with us as we make use of it. Prosper us in our new excursion. If it would do us harm to go up this mountain, if we would be puffed up with pride, if our souls or bodies would get any injury—frustrate our expedition. We desire to be as little children in Thy hands, going or staying, as it pleaseth Thee.'"

After giving many more touching illustrations of Mr. Hudson's simple, earnest, prayerful piety, Mr. McCormick proceeds to narrate the incidents of the mournful morning when he accompanied the party to seek the remains of his friend.

"We advanced slowly, and looked up at that awful precipice down which

THE ACCIDENT ON THE MATTERHORN.

they had fallen, and then shuddered to think how fearful a sight we were approaching. There was a pause before we reached them. The gentlemen first slowly drew near, and silently gazed at the sad spectacle they presented. The guides gathered round us. Croz and Hadow lay near together. Hudson was some distance behind. I recognised him. Almost the first thing found upon him was his Prayer-book—the very book out of which he had read to me a few days previously. I doubt not that he had turned to its pages the morning of the accident to procure nourishment for his soul. Whether the expedition which ended in his death was, in the eyes of worldly or religious people, wise or foolish, I am fully persuaded it was not undertaken without earnest prayer to God; and I am confident that he who loved to contemplate the beauties of the world, as God's good gifts, for the benefit and happiness of His children, must have been filled with joy and gratitude as he stood where no human being had ever stood before, and gazed from a new point of view on the great Creator's works. He had toiled up another Pisgah. A land of beauty lay before him. He looked upon this earthly Canaan as a type, beautiful but imperfect, of a heavenly country. Unconscious that his work in the desert of this world was done—that his pilgrimage here was fast drawing to a close—he began to descend. A few moments passed by, and angels came and carried him up in their hands—up to the Canaan of his hopes, the paradise of God.

"Before us lay, not the man, but the shattered tabernacle—the house of clay in which he had resided. *This* was not my Hudson. My friend was a regenerate soul. What I loved, studied, endeavoured to imitate, and was influenced by, was his spiritual nature. I had seen a frame as robust, a figure as perfect, a countenance as handsome, but never had I come in contact with a mind more heavenly—a spirit more Christ-like. That bruised body told me that he, like others, was a sinner; but I thought of him in his glorified state, above temptation, iniquity, and death—a saint in the blessed Saviour's presence. Such a scene as this makes the doctrine of the resurrection very precious; and the imagination tries to transform that broken, defaced, ruined frame which I saw lying beneath the Matterhorn, into a body like that of the Son of man, bearing His glorious name on the forehead, reflecting those rays which are above the brightness of the firmament, and as the stars; incorruptible and immortal; holy, perfect, beautiful.

"It was suggested that we should have a short funeral service. Poor Hudson's Prayer-book was produced for this purpose. I read out of it Psalm xc., so singularly appropriate to time and place, and repeated some prayers and a portion of the Burial Service. Imagine us standing, with our bronze-faced guides, leaning on their axes or alpenstocks around that newly-made and singular grave, in the centre of a snow-field, perhaps never before trodden by man, with that awful mountain frowning above us, under a cloudless sky—in the very sight, as it were, of the Almighty—and try and catch the sound of David's words: 'Lord, Thou hast been our refuge: from one generation to another. Before the mountains were brought forth, or ever the earth and the world were made: Thou art God from everlasting, and world without end. Thou turnest man to destruction: again Thou sayest, Come again, ye children of men.'"

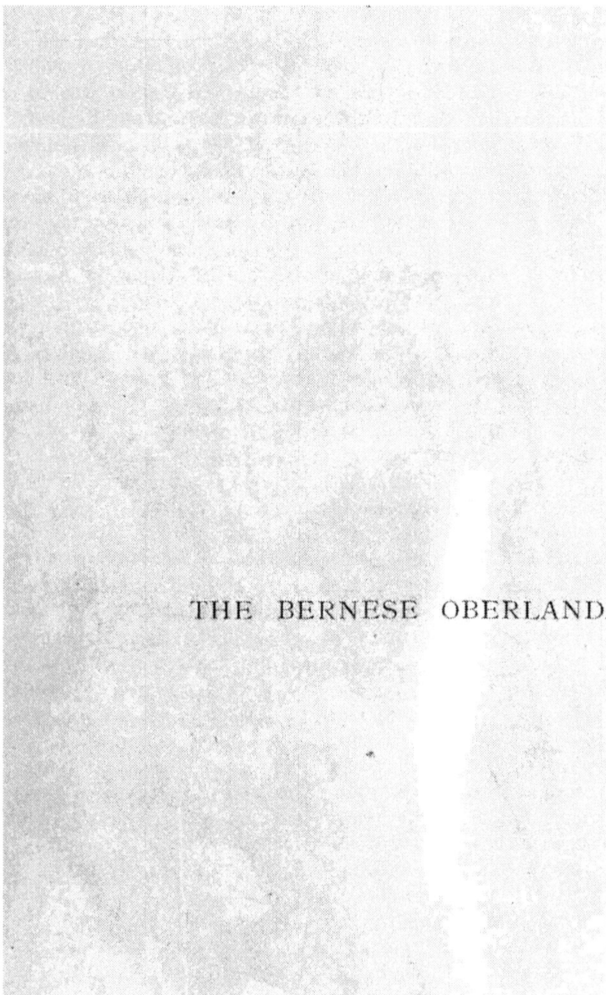

THE BERNESE OBERLAND.

ON THE TOP OF THE WETTERHORN.

The Bernese Oberland.

FROM ZERMATT TO THE OBERLAND—THE RHONE VALLEY—THE ÆGGISCHORN—THE ALETSCH GLACIER AND MARJELEN SEE—THE RHONE GLACIER AND THE GRIMSEL—HANDECK—MEYRINGEN—REICHENBACH—ROSENLAUI—THE WETTERHORN—THE WENGERN ALP—LAUTERBRUNNEN AND THE STAUBBACH—INTERLACHEN—THUN—BERNE—THE GEMMI AND LEUKERBAD.

THE valley of Zermatt is a *cul-de-sac,* closed at its upper end by the Matterhorn, the Breithorn, and their attendant giants, with one pass, the Col St. Théodule, which leads over snow and ice into the Val d'Aoste. Though this Col presents no difficulty to the stout pedestrian, it yet suffices to bar the head of the valley to the great majority of tourists, and leaves them no mode of exit except that by which they entered—the Nicolaithal to Stalden and Visp. This must be our route to the Bernese Oberland.

At Visp the Rhone Valley is reached, with its dirt and misery, its reeking, pestilential swamps and wretched, poverty-stricken villages, foul and fetid beyond expression. What Mr. Ruskin says of Sion will apply to all the towns of the Canton Valais. "It stands in the midst of a marshy valley, pregnant with various disease; the water either stagnant, or disgorged in wild torrents charged

VISP, AND VALLEY OF ZERMATT.

with earth; the air in the morning, stagnant also, hot, close, and infected; in the afternoon, rushing up from the outlet at Martigny in fitful and fierce whirlwind; one side of the valley in almost continual shade, the other scorched by the southern sun; while less traceable plagues than any of these bring on the inhabitants, at a certain time of life, violent affections of goitre, and often, in infancy, cretinism. Agriculture is attended with the greatest difficulties and despondencies: the land which the labour of a life has just rendered fruitful is often buried in an hour. Those who have not traversed the lower and central portions of the Rhone Valley can scarcely conceive the misery and squalor which

VIESCH, AND THE UPPER RHONE VALLEY.

appear on every hand. As we rise higher, however, the fogs and fens, the goitres and cretins, the filth and wretchedness disappear, and as we approach Viesch the people are brisker, the atmosphere clearer, the ground better cultivated."

It is a bright and joyful time in the close and oppressive valleys of Switzerland when the day arrives for driving the cattle to the mountain pastures, which from October to May are covered deep with snow. During the winter months the cattle are crowded together under cover, and not unfrequently the houses serve the purposes of stalls and stables. The châlet of many a wealthy farmer is divided between the flocks and herds, which occupy the ground-floor, and

OFF TO THE MOUNTAINS.

the owner and his family, who inhabit the middle storey, while the enormous attic serves as a hayloft. The Swiss peasant lives in happy unconsciousness of the stench which rises up through the floors and fills the house.

As spring advances and the sun gains power, the snow melts from the mountain pastures, and as it disappears, grass of a bright emerald green, enamelled with myriads of exquisite flowers, shoots forth and invites the herdman from the valley below. A procession is often formed, consisting of the inhabitants of the village, dressed in holiday clothes, and gay with ribbons, with which the animals are also decked; a band of music pours forth its enlivening strains, and the village pastor pronounces his benediction on the transactions of the day.

The cattle, who seem perfectly to understand what is going forward, appear almost frantic with joy at being released from their long imprisonment, and the procession moves upward to the high pasture ground on the mountain side, often at the distance of several miles from the village. The track thither winds through black and solemn pine forests, over roaring torrents, and not unfrequently across glaciers and snow fields. I once saw such a procession crossing the great Aletsch glacier, over the Upper Rhone Valley. On reaching the pasture ground, the cattle, each one bearing a bell, range at will over the flowery and fragrant turf; the herdsmen take up their abode for the summer in the mountain châlets, while their wives and families generally remain below. The cattle are driven in twice or thrice a day to be milked, and the processes of milking and cheese-making continue almost without interruption all the summer.

SUMMIT OF THE ÆGGISCHORN.

From Viesch an excellent mountain road leads to the hotel on the Æggischorn, where, at a height of seven thousand one hundred and fifty feet above the level of the sea, the traveller may enjoy a degree of comfort, and even luxury, perfectly wonderful in such a situation. The summit of the Æggischorn is between two and three thousand feet above the hotel, and may be easily reached in a couple of hours. There is a good path, practicable for ladies, all the way. The end of the climb, indeed, is rather a scramble, as the summit consists of masses of loose stones, and fragments of rock heaped confusedly on each other, like the summit of Cader Idris. The view is magnificent. Even

THE GREAT ALETSCH GLACIER.

if the ascent were ten times as difficult as it is the climber would be well rewarded for his toil.

In the ice-world of Switzerland there are few things more wonderful than the great Aletsch glacier at the foot of the Æggischorn. It rises, if we may apply such phraseology to a frozen river, in a vast basin of ice and snow, many miles in circumference, surrounded by huge peaks, which reach the height of from twelve to fourteen thousand feet. From this vast reservoir it flows forth for a course of fifteen or sixteen miles in length, and from one to two miles in width. Looked down upon from the Æggischorn or the Bell Alp, it is almost awful in its vastness and desolation. It may be doubted whether any glacier in Switzerland produces so profound an impression on the mind of the spectator. It is easily accessible along a great part of its extent, and some of the grandest peaks in the Oberland overhang it.

Another object of rare interest and beauty in this district is the Marjelen See—a lake about three miles long and half-a-mile broad, lying in a hollow on the flank of the Aletsch glacier. The head of the lake washes the glacier, which rises above it in steep ice-cliffs from twenty-five to fifty, or even sixty

THE MARJELEN LAKE AND ICE-CLIFFS OF THE ALETSCH GLACIER.

feet in height. The melting of these cliffs at the base, through the action of the water, causes huge boulders of ice to fall off into the lake below, in which they float like miniature icebergs. Its deep blue waters present an exquisite contrast to the glacier against which it rests. The contrast of colour is rendered yet more striking from the masses of ice floating in the lake.

The ordinary route from the Æggischorn to the Grimsel leads along the Upper Rhone Valley by Obergestelen. The scenery is not very interesting for Switzerland. It is pretty and pastoral in some places, wild and barren in others; but for the most part is unimpressive. Some grand views of the snowy dome of the Weisshorn are gained, however, which rescue the scenery from the imputation of being commonplace.

Approaching the Grimsel, the grand Rhone glacier comes into view. The ice-cave from which the infant Rhone leaps into life is of a stupendous size. The river bursts forth with a mighty roar, as though exulting at escape from its icy prison. "Down it rushes," says Cheever, "with the joy of liberty, swift and furious through the valley, leaping, dashing, thundering, foaming. Remembering the career it runs, how it sometimes floods the valleys like a sea, by how many rivers it is joined, how it pours dark and turbid into the Lake of Geneva, and

END OF GLACIER.

out again regenerated, clear as crystal, from Switzerland into France, and so into the Mediterranean, it is interesting to stand here, far above its mighty cradle, and look down upon its source. The glacier is a stupendous mass of ice-terraces clean across the valley, propped against an overhanging mountain, with snowy peaks towering to right and left. There is a most striking contrast between the bare desolation of the rocks on the Grimsel side and the grassy slopes of the mountains in companionship with this glacier. Your path lies along its margin, amidst a thick fringe of bushes and flowers, from which you can step down upon the roofs and walls of the ice-caverns, and look into the azure crevasses and hear the fall, the gurgle, the hurrying sub-glacial rush of unconscious streams, just born, as cold as death. Their first existence is in a symphony of dripping music, a prelude to the babble of the running rill, and then, as they grow older, they thunder with the roar of the cataract. Far above you, herds of cattle are seen browsing on the steep mountain-side—so steep, that it seems as if they must hold on to the herbage to keep from falling. The voices of the herdsmen echo down the valley; you half expect to see the whole group slide like an avalanche down into the glacier below."

The bushes and flowers to which Dr. Cheever refers are the red mountain rhododendrons, the Alpine roses, as they are sometimes called. They grow in great profusion in the higher Alps.* Nothing can be more beautiful than the flowers which flourish in the very drip of the glaciers. They are of the most brilliant colours, but commonly scentless. Switzerland is indeed the land of flowers. The pastures in the lowlands are bright with all the colours of the rainbow, and each zone, as we ascend, has its own distinctive flora, till we reach the height at which the rhododendron covers whole leagues of the mountain-side with its rich red blossoms. Higher still, the lichens and mosses, with their infinite varieties of tint, make the bleak bare rocks to glow with colour. Nowhere are the Alpine flowers more numerous, or their colours brighter, than on the slopes round the Rhone glacier; indeed, the neighbouring Alp takes its name, Mayenwand, from this circumstance.

The glacier itself is a fine example of what is called the fan-shaped glacier. Perhaps the comparison of a clenched fist would give a better idea of its form. The ice-stream pours down from a vast basin at the foot of the Galenstock, through a narrow gorge of rock. The part of the glacier shut in between these confined limits may be compared to the wrist. Escaping from the pressure of the enclosing walls of rock, the stream of ice expands, and the crevasses which seam and cleave the mass in its descent may represent the lines between the bones of the hand or of the fingers.

Ascending from the Rhone glacier toward the hospice, the traveller comes to one of the black, gloomy tarns, common enough in mountainous regions, but which never look so black and gloomy as when surrounded by the snow and ice of these Alpine passes. It is called the Todten See, or Lake of the Dead. The name is singularly appropriate, and in perfect keeping with the effect it produces upon the mind. The walls of rock around it are gloomy and bare; stern, sky-pointing peaks stand on every side in solemn majesty; the shores of the lake are destitute of vegetation, and its waters are black as night. No fish live in it; and it is said to be never frozen, even in the severest winters.

In the campaign between the French and Austrians (A.D. 1799), to which reference has already been made in the description of the Devil's Bridge, these Alpine solitudes, nine thousand feet above the level of the sea, were invaded by the storm of war. The Austrians had encamped and entrenched themselves here. Favoured by the advantages of their position, they had successfully

* The word "Alp" means, strictly, not the mountain, but the mountain pasture.

resisted all attempts to dislodge them. A peasant of Guttanen, seduced by the promise of a large reward, led a French column, by a secret pass across the mountains, upon the Austrian rear. Thus suddenly attacked from a quarter in which they believed themselves to be perfectly secure, they were seized with panic, and retreated in confusion, mowed down by a fusillade of French musketry. The bodies of the slain were thrown into the lake. The peasant lost his reward, and died in poverty.

The summit of the pass is a barren plateau, strewn with boulders. Here and there are beds of snow, which lie unmelted the whole year through. The track is indicated by a line of poles, which zigzag up the ascent and over the summit, adding to the general dreariness of the scene. Screened somewhat from the tempests, which howl and rave furiously over the pass, is the hospice. Once, like that on the St. Bernard, it was a monastery; now it is simply an inn, and like most Swiss inns in similar positions, it consists of a huge stone box, or ark, divided by slight wooden partitions into an innumerable multitude of cupboards, in each of which one or two beds are placed. The *salle-à-manger* is roughly fitted up, without much regard to comfort, and there are few nights in the year in which a fire is not acceptable. From November to March the hospice is occupied by only a single servant, supplied with provisions for the winter and with several dogs. Many stories of wild adventure and desperate danger are told of these lonely men during the months they are snowed up here.

However poor and inadequate the accommodation at the hospice may be, travellers arriving late in the afternoon have no alternative but to remain. There is no other shelter near, and the passes are too perilous to be traversed after nightfall. Some years ago I crossed the Grimsel in a furious thunder-storm. The rain poured down in torrents. It grew dark long before sunset, and for some time we were in imminent peril. At length we reached the desired shelter, to find every bed occupied. The only sleeping accommodation available was that afforded by the tables of the *salle-à-manger*. Five of these had been already engaged; three only remained, which we immediately applied for and secured. But guests continued to pour in. Amongst the new arrivals were several ladies, drenched to the skin, or, as one of them, with characteristic French exaggeration, declared, "to the very marrow of her bones." *Place aux dames!* We could not refuse to relinquish our tables under such circumstances as these. Twenty-five of us slept that night in the hayloft.

Many a droll scene is witnessed in the huts and châlets along the frequented routes when a storm bursts. Tourists pour in, till sometimes there is barely standing room. The ill-tempered grumbling of some, the good-humoured amusement of others, the shifts and devices resorted to by those who, having no change of raiment, are, in the French phrase, wet through to the marrow of their bones, and the queer costumes improvised, make up a scene not easily forgotten.

On the way from the Grimsel to Meyringen, by the Ober Hasli-thal, traces of bygone glacial action are distinctly visible, proving that at some former period the glaciers of Switzerland must have been far more extensive and numerous than at present. At one place the path leads past and over granite rocks polished smooth by the grinding motion of the ice, and cut into long deep grooves by the masses of stone which have been carried down by it. Nothing gives a more impressive sense of the immense force of glacial motion

ANY PORT IN A STORM.

than to observe how the hardest granite has been cut, as by a chisel. Similar striations are found in many parts of Europe. Notable examples have been pointed out on the rocks round Snowdon. But nowhere are they more obvious than between the Grimsel and Meyringen.

At Handeck, about five miles from the hospice, the falls of the Aar are

ROCKS POLISHED BY OLD GLACIERS.

passed. The river, after struggling through a narrow channel cut out of the solid rock, suddenly plunges over a rocky ledge into a dark chasm 200 feet deep. Another torrent, the Arlenbach, comes down from the opposite side of the ravine and makes it spring so that their waters meet in mid career. The din and fury of the falling torrents, the savage sublimity of the surrounding scenery, the gusts of wind that sweep up the narrow gorge, driving before them clouds of spray, and the rainbow spanning the falls, combine to make the scene one of rare grandeur.

From the Grimsel to Handeck the scenery, though very grand, is somewhat monotonous in its utter sterility. All is bleak and desolate. Vegetation seems annihilated, except in the forms of rhododendrons, mosses, and lichens. Crags scarred with tempests, peaks riven as by thunderbolts, torrents raging over their rocky beds, glaciers creeping down the mountain sides, fill the scene. But from Handeck downwards, the Ober Hasli-thal is transcendently beautiful. The river, rushing along swiftly and rejoicingly, makes music to the ear. The pine forests yield their grateful shade. Through frequent glades and openings the grand mountain-forms of the Bernese Oberland may be descried. Alpine flowers bloom in richest profusion. The combination of soft tender beauty with stern savage grandeur is most pleasing. There are few more agreeable memories of a tour in Switzerland than that of a fine day between Meyringen and the Grimsel.

We are exposed, however, in its full extent, to those pests of the Oberland —beggars, blowers of horns, firers of cannon, and sellers of fruit. At every turn the tourist is appealed to under one

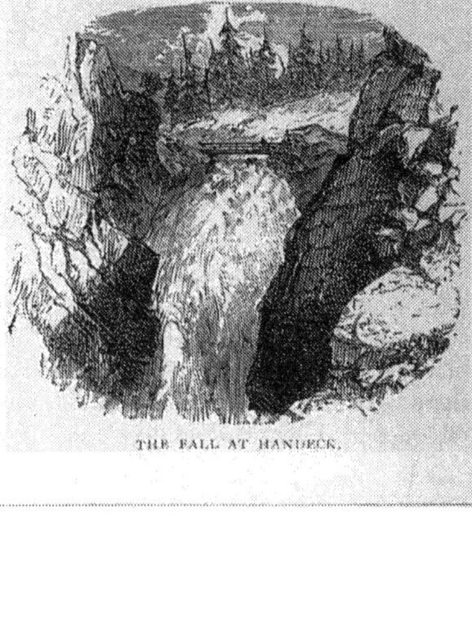

THE FALL AT HANDECK.

plea or another. Here a cretin mows and gibbers, holding out a dirty hand for an alms; there an old man shows a withered limb, or lifts his rags to disclose some frightful sore. Less disturbing to one's tranquillity, but still somewhat vexatious, are the constant invitations to hear some wonderful echo. At the most favourable points on the road men or boys station themselves, provided with huge Alpine cow-horns four or five feet in length, or with a dangerous-looking cannon, honeycombed, rusty, and, apparently, loaded to the very teeth. It must be admitted, however, that these echoes are often singularly beautiful. One of Wordsworth's finest sonnets describes and moralises upon the effect produced by the echoes on the Gemmi:

ECHO UPON THE GEMMI.

"WHAT beast of chase hath broken from the cover?
Stern GEMMI listens to as full a cry,
As multitudinous a harmony
Of sound as rang the heights of Latmos over,
When, from the soft couch of her sleeping lover,
Up-starting, Cynthia skimmed the mountain-dew
In keen pursuit—and gave, where'er she flew,
Impetuous motion to the stars above her.
A solitary wolf-dog, ranging on
Through the bleak concave, wakes this wondrous chime
Of aëry voices locked in unison,—
Faint—far off—near—deep—solemn and sublime!—
So, from the body of one guilty deed,
A thousand ghostly fears and haunting thoughts proceed!"

The Grimsel marks the division between the Catholic cantons of Southern Switzerland and the Protestant cantons of the north. Again the contrast in the moral, social, and religious influence of the two forms of faith is forced upon us. That the comparison is altogether favourable to Protestantism cannot be doubted. It is even admitted by the Romanists themselves. Leaving the Vallais with its squalor and wretchedness, and crossing the pass into this bright cheerful valley, where everything seems thriving and prosperous, is like passing from the most poverty-stricken districts of Ireland into Devonshire or Surrey. The partisan of Rome may endeavour to explain away the inference, but he cannot deny the fact. "We have cantons whose frontiers interlock with one another as do my fingers," said M. Sismondi, to a friend of the writer's, clasping his hands and interlacing his fingers as he spoke, "and you need not to be told—a glance suffices to show you—whether you are in a Protestant or a Catholic canton." To the same gentleman a catholic priest admitted the fact, but, with great *naïveté*, explained it by saying, "The good God knows that you heretics have no hope for another world, so He gives you some compensation in this!" Even so zealous a Catholic and so accomplished a writer as M. Raoul Rochette says, "Generally, as in Glaris and Appenzell, the Catholics have continued to be shepherds, whilst the Protestants have turned their attention to trade or manufactures. The poverty of the former contrasts with the affluence of the latter, so that, at first sight, it would seem to be better in this world to live with the Protestants than the Catholics; *but there is another world, in which this inferiority is probably compensated.*"

The Reichenbach Falls form the chief attraction at Meyringen. I know no spot where the tourist can better study the arrowy character of a waterfall. The stream here is considerable, and it takes a fine buoyant header off a shelf of rock upon the hard stone floor of the chasm below. Of course it bursts and splashes off all round with much noise, and flings so much spray up the sides of the basin into which it leaps as to supply material for a number of baby falls, which run back like young ones to their parent. But its arrowy character is its most striking feature. It is like a sheaf of water-rockets rushing downwards. The moment the stream leaps clear off the rock it begins to form these barbed shoots.

FRUIT SELLER AND HORN BLOWER.

The landlord of the hotel at the foot of the Falls treats his guests to a grand illumination of them on certain evenings in the week. The effect struck me as being unexpectedly fine. It cannot be better described than in the words of *The Times* correspondent: "The air was mild and still, and the darkness of the hour was hardly relieved in that hollow gorge by the few stars twinkling overhead. The hour was well chosen: heaven and earth were propitious, and when the signal-rocket flashed in the air, the soul of every bystander was thoroughly ripened for the coming wonder by those few minutes of trembling expectation. The rocket flashed up, the Bengal lights blazed out—red lights, green lights, violet lights. First the dark firs and the russet and gold beech-bushes were all on fire, then the waters gleamed out, rill after rill, blushing in the red, smiling in the green, fainting in the violet beams. A rich, warm life rushed from end to end all along that heaving stream—rich, warm life, where, one second before, there was only blank stillness and gloom. Rapid and fitful the ever-changing hues flitted up and down the successive leaps of the Fall; and calm, and pure, and solemn the silver tide poured down, unmoved in its perpetual flow, swelling its smooth arches, flashing on its hollow rock-beds, as unconcerned in all that glory of light as if it were only basking in its wonted sunbeams, or

FALLS OF THE REICHENBACH.

reflecting the pale glimmer of the genial moon. The effect was magical. The flood of those coloured lights did not merely flutter here and there on the surface of the waters; it went through their liquid mass from the rocky paths in their rear, shone through it as through the purest crystal, setting off each foaming billow, as one pressed upon the other in endless succession, imparting animation to the whole pillar of water, as if living things, tritons or water-nymphs, had been floating up and down beneath that smooth compact surface—vague nondescript beings dancing and fluttering, likes motes in a sunbeam. The effect was magical, not to be forgotten by any one who has seen it; worth seeing at the cost of much money, and ever so much trouble. All my theories on the true and false beautiful in art and nature were blown to the ground, and as the light faded away, and the waterfall was replunged into its nocturnal darkness, I had to avow that I had been delighted in spite of my preconceptions, charmed in defiance of my better reason."

THE STREET OF MEYRINGEN.

The cheerful and thriving village of Meyringen is the centre upon which eight or nine mountain passes converge. It is therefore a favourite halting-place for tourists on Sunday, being readily accessible and possessing excellent accommodation. English service is now conducted in the church erected for that purpose, instead of the Lutheran church, the use of which had previously been granted by the authorities.

The scenery all along the road from Meyringen to Grindelwald is magnificent. The peaks of the Oberland are in view the whole day. The Englehorn, the Wellhorn, the Shreckhorn, the Eigher, replace one another as the road winds along.* Approaching Grindelwald the huge masses of the Wetterhorn seem absolutely to overhang the path. The glaciers which stream down through the dark pine woods to the bright green pastures of the valley complete a scene of surpassing loveliness and grandeur.

Nothing would seem more futile than the attempt to scale these peaks. They appear absolutely and hopelessly inaccessible. Mr. Ball says of the Shreckhorn:

* The names of many of these mountains are very suggestive; the Angel's Peak, the peaks of Tempest, of Darkness, and of Terror, the Silver Peak, and the Virgin.

"On three sides the rocks are so steep as to be almost completely bare of snow; the north alone shows a long slope of snow lying at the highest possible angle, and in such a condition that the slightest disturbance is apt to cause avalanches." Again, "The Ober Grindelwald glacier, whether seen from the Faulhorn, from the neighbourhood of the village, or from any other commanding spot, presents an aspect which may well make the boldest mountaineer hesitate. The glacier is in truth an almost continuous ice-fall, torn by wide crevasses into toppling ridges and pinnacles of ice. When the eye turns from the glacier to the mountains on either side, with the hope of tracing a passage, the prospect is at first sight even more discouraging. The precipices of the Wetterhorn on one side, and those of the Mettenberg on the other, rise in walls of rock so steep and, seemingly, so unbroken, that it is hard to conceive how even a chamois could make its way along them. The experienced cragsman, however, knows that the steepest rocks are almost always broken by ravines and gullies, and traversed by narrow ledges that give foothold to the skilful climber." Again, "The summit of the Wetterhorn rises little more than 800 feet above this Col, but the slope is so extremely steep that from one to two hours must be allowed for the ascent. The slope increases from 50° to 58° towards the summit. This consists of a perilously sharp crest of frozen snow, running for a short distance N. and S., which, when reached by Mr. Wills, was topped by an overhanging cornice of ice. It is only by levelling the summit with an axe that space enough for a seat can be found on this dizzy eminence."* Yet all these peaks have been ascended, "even that grimmest fiend of the Oberland, the Shreckhorn." Judgments differ as to the expediency—some even doubt the morality—of these perilous ascents. Reckless risking of life cannot, for a moment, be justified. But no one can withhold his admiration from the qualities demanded for success. The mountaineer, to accomplish such feats as these, must possess coolness, courage, readiness of resource, a determination which no difficulties can daunt, pluck which no dangers can appal. Nor are the merely physical qualifications required—the firm foot, the strong arm, the endurance of cold and hunger and fatigue, the power of walking on the edge of a precipice without dizziness, or climbing a snow-slope without exhaustion—to be altogether despised.

Passing Grindelwald, the road leads over the Wengern Alp. Approached from this side, the ascent is gradual, and for the most part bare and treeless. The summit of the pass is 6280 feet above the level of the sea. Beneath is a broad, deep valley, on the opposite side of which rise the giants of the Bernese Oberland:—the Jungfrau, 13,671 feet in height; the Monch, 13,438; the Eigher, 13,044; the Shreckhorn, 13,386; the Finster Aarhorn, 14,039. Murray tells us that the glaciers which cling round these peaks and fill up the depressions between them extend without interruption from the Jungfrau to the Grimsel, and from Grindelwald, in canton Berne, nearly to Brieg, in the Vallais. The extent of this glacier has been calculated at 115 square miles.

* The *Alpine Guide—Central Alps*. By John Ball, late President of the Alpine Club.

THE WELLHORN AND WETTERHORN.

Cheever, who ascended from the other side, says of the view :—"As we wind our way up the steep side of the mountain, the mists are slowly and gracefully rising from the depths of the valley along the face of the outjutting crags. It seems as if the genius of nature were drawing a white soft veil around her bosom. But now as we rise still farther, the sun, pouring its fiery rays against the opposite mountain, makes it seem like a smoking fire begirt with clouds. You think of Mount Sinai all in a blaze with the glory of the steps of Deity. The very rocks are burning and the green forests also. Then there are the white glittering masses of the Breithorn and the Mittaghorn in the distance, and a cascade shooting directly out from the glacier. Upwards the mists are still curling and hanging to the mountains, while below there are the clumps of trees in the sunlight, the deep exquisite green of spots of unveiled meadow, the winding stream, now hid and now revealed, the grey mist sleeping on the tender grass, the châlets shining, the brooks murmuring, the birds singing, the sky above and the earth beneath, in this 'incense-breathing morn' uniting in a universal harmony of beauty and melody of praise.

'In such a season of calm weather,
Though inland far we be,
Our souls have sight of that immortal sea
Which brought us hither;
Can in a moment travel thither,—
And see the children sport upon the shore,
And hear the mighty waters rolling evermore !'

"And now we pass on, and enter a silent sea of pines, how beautiful ! silent, still, solemn, religious ; dark against the enormous snowy masses and peaks before us. How near their glittering glaciers seem upon us ! How clear the atmosphere ! How our voices ring out upon it, and the very hum of the insects in the air is distinctly sonorous ! We have now ascended to such a height that we can look across the vales and mountains, down into Unterseen and Interlachen. And now before us rises the Jungfrau Alp, how sublimely ! But at this moment of the view, the Silberhorn is far more lovely, with its fields of dazzling snow, than the Jungfrau, which here presents a savage perpendicular steep, a wall of rock, scarred and seamed indeed, but so steep that the snow and ice cannot cling to its jagged points. Higher up commence the tremendous glaciers, presenting a chaos of enormous ravines of snow and ice, just ready to topple down the ridge of the mountain.

"When we come to the inn upon the Wengern Alp we are nearly 5500 feet above the level of the sea. We are directly in face of the Jungfrau, upon whose masses of perpetual snow we have been gazing with so much interest. They seem close to us, so great is the deception in clear air, but a deep, vast ravine (I know not but a league across from where we are) separates the Wengern Alp from the Jungfrau, which rises in an abrupt sheer precipice, of many thousand feet, somewhat broken into terraces, down which the avalanches, from the higher beds of untrodden everlasting snow, plunge thundering into the uninhabitable abyss. Perhaps there is not another mountain so high in all Switzerland, which you can look at so near and so full in the face. Out of this ravine the Jungfrau rises 11,000 feet, down which vast height the avalanches sometimes sweep with their incalculable masses of ice from the very topmost summit.

"The idea of a mass of ice so gigantic that it might overwhelm whole hamlets, or sweep away a forest in its course, being shot down, with only one or two interruptions, a distance of 11,000 feet, is astounding. But it is those very interruptions that go to produce the overpowering sublimity of the scene. Were there no concussion intervening between the loosening of the mountain ridge of ice and snow, and its fall into the valley, if it shot sheer off into the air, and came down in one solid mass unbroken, it would be as if a mountain had fallen at noonday out of heaven. And this would certainly be sublime in the highest degree, but it would not have the awful slowness and deep prolonged roar of the Jungfrau avalanche in mid air, nor the repetition of sublimity with each interval of thousands of feet, in which it strikes and thunders.

"I think that without any exception it was the grandest sight I ever beheld, not even the cataract of Niagara having impressed me with such thrilling sublimity. Ordinarily, in a sunny day at noon, the avalanches are falling on the Jungfrau about every ten minutes, with the roar of thunder, but they are seldom visible, and sometimes the traveller crosses the Wengern Alp without witnessing them at all. But we were so very highly favoured as to see two of the grandest avalanches possible in the course of about an hour, between twelve o'clock and two. One cannot command any language to convey an adequate idea of their magnificence.

"You are standing far below, gazing up to where the great disc of the glittering Alp cuts the heavens, and drinking in the influence of the silent scene around. Suddenly an enormous mass of snow and ice, in itself a mountain, seems to move; it breaks from the toppling outmost mountain ridge of snow, where it is hundreds of feet in depth, and in its first fall of perhaps 2000 feet is broken into millions of fragments. As you first see the flash of distant artillery by night, then hear the roar, so here you may see the white flashing mass majestically bowing, then hear the astounding din. A cloud of dusty, misty, dry snow rises into the air from the concussion, forming a white volume of fleecy smoke, or misty light, from the bosom of which thunders forth the icy torrent in its second prodigious fall over the rocky battlements. The eye follows it delighted, as it ploughs through the path which preceding avalanches have worn, till it comes to the brink of a vast ridge of bare rock, perhaps more than 2000 feet perpendicular. Then pours the whole cataract over the gulf, with a still louder roar of echoing thunder, to which nothing but the noise of Niagara in its sublimity is comparable.

"Nevertheless, you may think of the tramp of an army of elephants, of the roar of multitudinous cavalry marching to battle, of the whirlwind tread of 10,000 bisons sweeping across the prairie, of the tempest surf of ocean beating and shaking the continent, of the sound of torrent floods or of a numerous host, or of the voice of the trumpet on Sinai, exceeding loud, and waxing louder and louder, so that all the people in the camp trembled, or of the rolling orbs of that fierce chariot described by Milton,

> 'Under whose burning wheels,
> The steadfast empyrean shook throughout.'

It is with such a mighty shaking tramp that the avalanche thunders down.

"Another fall of still greater depth ensues, over a second similar castellated ridge or reef in the face of the mountain, with an awful, majestic slowness, and a tremendous crash in its concussion, awakening again the reverberating peals of thunder. Then the torrent roars on to another smaller fall, till at length it reaches a mighty groove of snow and ice. Here its progress is slower, and last of all you listen to the roar of the falling fragments, as they drop, out of sight, with a dead weight into the bottom of the gulf, to rest there for ever.

"Now figure to yourself a cataract like that of Niagara (for I should judge the volume of one of these avalanches to be probably every way superior in bulk to the whole of the Horse-shoe Fall), poured in foaming grandeur, not merely over one great precipice of 200 feet, but over the successive ridgy precipices of 2000 or 3000, in the face of a mountain 11,000 feet high, and tumbling, crashing, thundering down, with a continuous din of far greater sublimity than the sound of the grandest cataract. Placed on the slope of the Wengern Alp, right opposite the whole visible side of the Jungfrau, we have enjoyed two of these mighty spectacles, at about half an hour's interval between them. The first was the most sublime, the second the most beautiful. The roar of the falling mass begins to be heard the moment it is loosened from the mountain; it pours on with the sound of a vast body of rushing water; then comes the first great concussion, a booming crash of thunder breaking on the still air of mid-heaven; your breath is suspended as you listen and look; the mighty glittering mass shoots headlong over the main precipice, and the fall is so great that it produces to the eye that impression of dread majestic slowness, of which I have spoken, though it is doubtless more rapid than Niagara. But if you should see the cataract of Niagara itself coming down 5000 feet above you in the air, there would be the same impression. The image remains in the mind, and can never fade from it; it is as if you had seen an alabaster cataract from heaven.

"The sound is far more sublime than that of Niagara, because of the preceding stillness in those awful Alpine solitudes. In the midst of such silence and solemnity, from out the bosom of those glorious glittering forms of nature, comes that rushing, crashing thunder-burst of sound. If it were not that your soul, through the eye, is as filled and fixed with the sublimity of the vision, as through the sense of hearing with that of the audible report, methinks you would wish to bury your face in your hands, and fall prostrate, as at the voice of the Eternal! But it is impossible to convey any adequate idea of the combined impression made upon the soul by these rushing masses and rolling thunders. When you see the smaller avalanches, they are of the very extreme of beauty, like jets of white powder, or heavy white mist or smoke, poured from crag to crag, as if the Staubbach itself were shot from the top of the Jungfrau."

Continuing our journey across the Wengern, the road gradually loses the barrenness and sterility which characterise the Grindelwald side, and plunges downward through pine woods and luxuriant pastures and well-kept farms, into the valley of Lauterbrunnen. The numerous châlets which stud the mountain-side

INSIDE THE CHÂLET.

add greatly to the picturesqueness of the scenery. The pine wood of which they are constructed acquires a rich brown colour from smoke and exposure to the atmosphere. They contrast finely with the bright emerald green of the pastures, or the savage rocks, and black gloomy forests overhead. But, like many other things in this world, they are more pleasing at a distance than close at hand. The dirt and disorder of the interior may vie with those of the meanest Irish cabin;

and many a wealthy farmer, whose home in the valley beneath is furnished with every comfort, will spend the weeks of summer in a wretched *Senhütte*, which we in England should think hardly fit for a dog-kennel. The soil outside is trampled

OUTSIDE THE CHÂLET.

ankle deep in mire, with patches of overgrown nettles and docks, which grow in rank luxuriance. The traveller, too, must be on his guard against the savage dogs which are often left to guard the huts during the absence of the inmates.

More than once I have felt myself in considerable peril from these untamed brutes; nor is it safe to reckon with absolute confidence on the friendly disposition of the numerous bulls which wander round the huts.

SWISS COWHERD.

The tourist will hardly fail to notice a somewhat strange phenomenon in the cowherds on the mountain-side. At a distance they seem to be furnished with stout, well-proportioned tails. Was, then, Lord Monboddo right? Are we descended from a race furnished with these caudal appendages? Or is this a species of the genus Man, which we may dub *Homo caudatus?* Theories about the origin of the race have been rife of late years, and very slight and doubtful have been the facts which have served as their basis. Many a proud edifice of speculation has risen to a towering height on foundations as slender as the tails of the milkmen on the slopes of the Wengern. See! they proceed to sit down upon their tails; and very comfortable stools they prove. The mystery is solved. The tails are one-legged stools which the owners carry strapped round them, *in situ*, so that both hands are left free—one to carry the milking-pail, the other to help in climbing the mountain-side, a provision very needful on such slopes as these.

The name of the valley into which we descend, Lauterbrunnen, means *Nothing but fountains.* Few names could be more appropriate and descriptive. Innumerable streamlets, after careering for some time out of sight on the higher Alps, spring over the abrupt cliffs and buttresses of rock, or leap down the smooth grassy slopes which inclose this delicious valley, reaching the bottom in showers of spray. When mists rest upon the surrounding mountains, as is often the case, the effect is very curious; the cascades seem to dangle from the clouds, hanging like long skeins of silver thread over the perpendicular cliffs. The supreme beauty of these falls is only seen in the forenoon of a bright day, when the waving spray of each is changed into a shower of rainbows.

The principal cascade in the valley is the Staubbach, that is, *The dustfall.* It takes its name from the fact that in the course of its descent the whole mass of water is beaten into spray, and falls to the ground like a shower of diamond dust. It is the loftiest fall in Europe, springing over the perpendicular face of the cliff at

THE STAUBBACH AND VALLEY OF LAUTERBRUNNEN.

a height of 900 feet from the ground. In speaking of the Isola Bella, reference was made to the conflicting opinions expressed respecting its beauty. There is no less difference of judgment as to the Staubbach. A German writer has compared the Reichenbach to a wild irregular ode, the Giesbach to an epic, the fall at Handeck to a sublime hymn, and the Staubbach to a fairy tale. Wordsworth calls it,

"This bold, this pure, this sky-born waterfall."

Byron writes,

"The sunbow's rays still arch
The torrent with the many hues of heaven,
And roll the sheeted silver's waving column
O'er the crags headlong perpendicular,

And fling its lines of foaming light along,
And to and fro, like the pale courser's tail,
The giant steed, to be bestrode by Death,
As told in the Apocalypse."

Murray compares it to a beautiful lace veil, suspended from the cliffs above, waving over the face of the mountain. Cheever says of it: "It is the most exquisitely beautiful of waterfalls, though there are miniatures of it in the Valley of the Arve almost as beautiful. You have no conception of the volume of water, nor of the grandeur of the fall, until you come near it, almost beneath it; but its extreme beauty is better seen and felt at a little distance; indeed we thought it looked more beautiful than ever when we saw it, about ten o'clock, from the mountain ridge on the opposite side of the valley. It is nearly 900 feet in height, over the perpendicular precipice, so that the eye traces its course so long, and its movement is so checked by the resistance of the air and the roughness of the mountain, that it seems rather to float than to fall, and before it reaches the bottom, dances down in ten thousand little jets of white foam, which all alight together, as softly as a white-winged albatross on the bosom of the ocean. It is as if a million of rockets were shot off in one shaft into the air, and then descended together, some of them breaking at every point in the descent, and all streaming down in a combination of meteors. So the streams in this fall, where it springs into the air, separate and hold their own as long as possible, and then burst into rockets of foam, dropping down at first heavily, as if determined to reach the ground unbroken, and then dissolving into showers of mist, so gracefully, so beautifully, like snow-dust on the bosom of the air, that it seems like a spiritual creation rather then a thing inert, material."

FALL NEAR LAUTERBRUNNEN.

There is no doubt that the beauty of the fall varies at various times. In a wet season or after a copious rainfall it is a very striking object. But when a long drought has yet further diminished the small quantity of water which ordinarily comes over the mountain side the effect is disappointing. It is said that in winter, when the torrent is nearly arrested by frost, colossal icicles are formed, many hundred feet in length, some hanging down from above, others rising up, like enormous stalagmites, from beneath.

A delightful walk, of about three hours, along the banks of the Lutschine, brings the tourist to Interlachen. The valley of Lauterbrunnen should, however, be traversed in the opposite direction. In ascending from Interlachen the scenery increases in grandeur, and the snowy peaks of the Jungfrau are continually in view, advantages which are lost in descending from the Wengern Alp.

THE JUNGFRAU, FROM INTERLACHEN.

Interlachen is the head-quarters of dilettante tourists, who go abroad because other people do so, and because London and Paris are dull in the autumn. The late president of the Alpine Club, as might be expected, pours out his scorn upon the denizens of this "chosen resort of those strangers who desire to carry with them into the sanctuary of Nature as much as possible of the habits of fashionable watering-place society. Incapable of deriving deep and continuous enjoyment from the sublime objects around them, a large portion of the visitors of the gentle sex find constant occupation in the display of city finery; while the less fortunate male idlers are too often reduced to a condition of utter vacuity, provoking painful

CASTLE OF SPIETZ, LAKE OF THUN.

comparisons between their condition and that of Dr. Guggenbuhl's patients on the Abendberg." Mr. Ball admits, however, that, "in spite of these disturbing elements, a stranger whose temper they do not ruffle" may spend some delightful days or even weeks here. Interlachen is certainly placed in the midst of some of the most beautiful scenery of Switzerland, and it affords an admirable centre from which innumerable excursions may be made.

Interlachen takes its name from lying between the two lakes of Brientz and Thun. Our course will lead us across the latter. If it lacks the solemn grandeur of the Lake of Lucerne or the exquisite beauty of that of Como, it yet possesses a combination of the two, which, in the judgment of many tourists, makes it not unworthy to rank with them. The banks are gay with thriving villages and picturesque châlets. The grand masses of the Niesen and the Stockhorn occupy the foreground, and noble views are gained of the snow-crowned summits of the Monch and Eigher in the distance. Legends innumerable linger about the shores of the lake. Tradition connects the castle of Spietz, on a projecting tongue of land at the foot of the Niesen, with the terrible Attila and his Huns. St. Beatus, the first missionary to this district, is reported to have dispensed with the services of boat and boatmen, simply spreading his cloak on the lake when he sailed across it. A huge dragon which had devastated the country for some years, and which no one dared to attack, occupied a cave on the mountain side overhanging the lake. St. Beatus desired to deliver the neighbourhood from this pest, and at the same time coveted the dragon's den for himself. By simply giving

COSTUME OF SWISS GIRLS.

the monster notice to quit he achieved both objects. The dragon, it is said, took his departure when bidden, and the saint entered upon the vacant cave.

Few, if any, towns in Switzerland are more picturesque or more pleasantly situated than Thun. The views from its environs extend across the blue waters of the lake, across the narrow strip of orchard and garden on its shores, up to the oak forests, up to the pine forests, up to the bright green pastures dotted with châlets, up to the bare mountain sides, up to the belt of snow, up to the peaks of the Monch, the Eigher, the Jungfrau in mid-air, up to the deep azure above. Nowhere are there richer combinations and more striking contrasts of form and colour. The architecture of the town is quaint and antique in style. The narrow streets, projecting gables, carved timbers, and rude frescoes present many subjects for the antiquarian or the artist.

At no great distance from Thun is Berne, the seat of the Federal Government, and the capital of the most powerful canton in the confederacy. It is a thriving city, and, in the process of rebuilding, is rapidly losing its most picturesque features. Indeed, all that is characteristic both in architecture and dress is being "improved off the face of the earth." National and cantonal costumes are disappearing. The shop windows still display pictures of the dresses of the cantons, but many of them are rarely to be seen in real life. Here and there one comes upon a group of girls chatting round a fountain, dressed in a style which recalls the days of Swiss pastoral simplicity when *modes* from Paris were unknown. But such sights are becoming rarer every year, and threaten, before long, to vanish from the towns altogether.

The Bear, which is the crest of Berne, appears everywhere. There is a bear-pit outside the town, in which several of these animals are kept at the cost of the government. An English gentleman fell into it a few years ago and was killed by them. The great clock-tower in the middle of the town is fitted up with machinery which moves a procession of puppet-bears every hour. The fountains are all surmounted by bears—rampant, couchant, and courant—in iron and bronze, stone and wood. One is clad in complete armour, with breast-plate, thigh-pieces, and helmet, a sword by his side and a banner in his paws.

The Swiss Confederation, of which Berne is the Federal capital, consists of twenty-two cantons, each of which manages its own internal affairs, delegating certain carefully-defined powers to the central government. Its constitution is thus similar to that of the United States of America. The federal-pact was settled in the year 1815, when the Allied Powers recognised the independence of the Republic at the Congress of Vienna. It was agreed that the Diet should meet once a year, at Berne, Zurich, and Lucerne alternately, to discuss and decide all questions affecting the common interests of the confederation, reserving to each canton internal independence. The Diet was empowered to conduct all foreign negotiations and alliances, to make peace and war, and to appoint envoys to foreign states. A majority of three-fourths of the whole was required for the declaration of war or peace. In other cases a simple majority was sufficient.

Each canton had a single vote. The cantons were prohibited from taking up arms against each other, but all internal differences were to be referred for settlement to the Federal Diet. This was a most important clause in the pact, as the incessant feuds between the different cantons had, previously, been the cause of frequent and interminable wars. The war of the Sonderbund a few years ago proves the value

HIGH STREET, BERNE.

and necessity of this stipulation. In case of serious disturbances within any one of the cantons, the Diet was authorised, under certain well-defined conditions, to mediate between the contending parties and, if necessary, to prevent violence by military occupation. The Federal intervention, in the autumn of 1865, in the city and canton of Geneva, will be remembered by most readers. When the Diet separated for the year it was to give instructions to the Vorort, or directing canton, to carry out the measures agreed upon, and provide for the well-being of the confederacy until its next meeting. The Vorort was to be guided and aided in discharging the duties entrusted to it by a Federal chancery appointed by the Diet. In case of need, or on the demand of five cantons, the Vorort was authorised to convoke an extraordinary meeting of the Diet.

The war of the Sonderbund, brought about by the intrigues of the Jesuits, rendered a revision of the constitution necessary. After lengthened discussion this was completed in 1848. The general principles of the federal-pact of 1815 were retained unaltered, but changes were introduced designed to confer greater unity, strength, and freedom of action on the central government. This was effected by restricting the powers previously possessed by the cantons, and increasing those of the Diet. Each canton had coined its own money, levied its own customs-duties, and regulated its own passport system. These functions were now transferred to the Federal Government. The members of the Diet had hitherto been only delegates recording the decision of their constituents, to whom they had to refer for instructions how to act in every emergency. Since 1848 greater responsibility and liberty of action has been exercised by the members, as in the English representative system. The sittings of the Diet no longer alternate between different cities, but are held uniformly in Berne. The new constitution is found to work well, and even those cantons which most vehemently opposed the change are now satisfied with its operation.

CATHEDRAL AND PLATFORM AT BERNE.

In the internal government of each canton frequent changes occur, and great diversities of political organisation prevail. In some the constitution is democratic, and the cantonal government is chosen by universal suffrage. In others the aristocratic element is still retained. But the briefest summary of the various political systems existing in the several cantons would require far more space than we have at our disposal.

The view from the platform of the cathedral, or the Enghi Promenade, is, to tourists, the great glory of Berne. In clear weather the whole range of the Bernese Oberland can be descried. Many competent judges, Humboldt amongst the number, have classed this amongst the very finest views in Europe. The Wetterhorn, the Shreckhorn, the Finster-Aarhorn, the Eigher, the Monch, the Jungfrau, the Gletscherhorn, the Mittaghorn, the Blumlis Alp, the Niesen, and the Stockhorn are all in sight. Nowhere is the rosy blush of sunrise and sunset upon the snowy peaks more delicately beautiful. It is necessary, however, that the atmosphere be perfectly clear. From the great distance over which the eye must range, a slight haze is sufficient to intercept the view.

Returning from Berne to Thun, and proceeding thence to the Gemmi and Leukerbad, the road leads first along the beautiful shores of the Lake of Thun, and then through a rich pastoral valley studded with picturesque villages and thriving farmsteads. But for the dress of the peasantry, and the peculiar style of architecture everywhere adopted, many parts of the valley of Frutigen might lead the traveller to forget that he was in Switzerland, and to fancy himself in one of the most fertile and best-farmed counties of England. As Kandersteg is approached, the ascent becomes more rapid, and the scenery assumes an Alpine character.

Leaving Kandersteg, the path, after a steep ascent, traverses a bleak, bare plateau, and winds round a desolate gloomy tarn, the Dauben See, whose ice-cold waters are fed by the melting of the Lammeren glacier. A little way farther and the path seems to terminate on the brink of a tremendous precipice—a wall of perpendicular rock, 2000 feet from base to summit. This is the far-famed Gemmi Pass. The superb view of the Monte Rosa chain bursts upon the eye with almost startling suddenness. The whole range, from the Mischabelhorner to the Dent Blanche, are perfectly visible, including Monte Rosa and the Matterhorn. It used to be asserted that Monte Rosa was not visible, being masked by some intervening peaks. It is now, however, generally admitted that the queen of the Alps does come into the line of view.

But how to reach the village of Leukerbad is the question. It lies 2000 feet below us: the huge hotels looking like toy-houses in the distance. The bastions of rock are perpendicular: in some places they even overhang the valley. Yet down the face of this scarped rock must we descend. From below a few men and mules may be seen making their way upward or downward, and looking like flies clinging to the bare surface of the rock. They are passing over a perfectly good road, made in the course of last century by a party of Tyrolese work-people, who have turned the gorge of the Dala from being a mere *cul de sac* into one of the most frequented passes in the Alps. Availing themselves of a deep cleft running from top to bottom of the wall of rock, these ingenious and daring, though uneducated, engineers formed a series of zigzags up the sides of the chasm, and thus have constructed a winding staircase of about five feet in width, which forms a perfectly practicable road. The track is protected on the outer side by a low wall or railings, and is quite safe for pedestrians. There is little or no danger in riding up the pass; but to ride down is sheer madness. A year or two ago a French lady was thrown over the head of her mule and dashed to pieces as she made the rash attempt. The cantonal authorities now require all persons to dismount at the top and walk down.

Leukerbad, at the foot of the Gemmi, is a village crowded to overflowing during a few weeks of summer, and deserted all the rest of the year. It consists almost exclusively of huge hotels and bath-houses. During the season large numbers of visitors assemble here, of whom a minority come for the enjoyment of

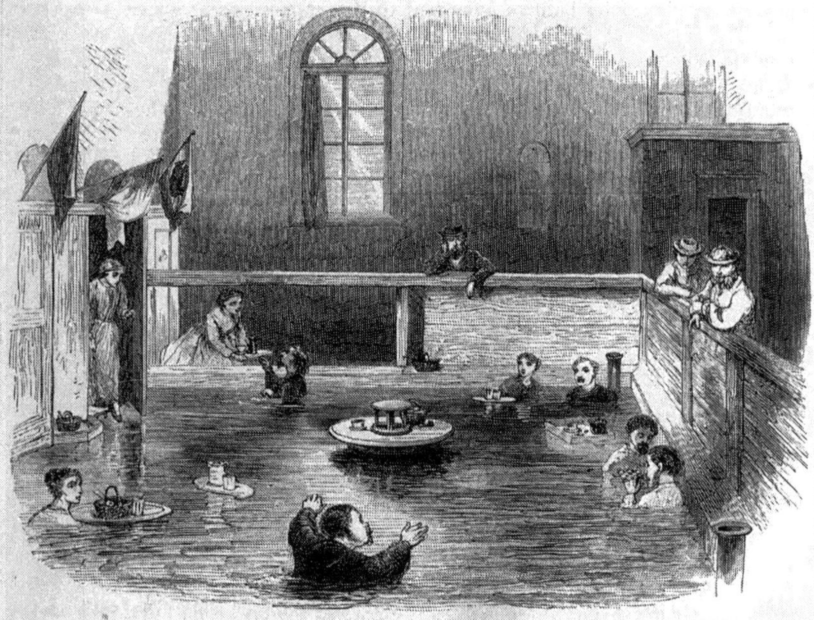

THE BATHS AT LEUKERBAD.

the magnificent scenery of the neighbourhood, and the majority for the famous hot baths. There are ten or twelve springs which burst forth in and around the valley. The supply of hot mineral water is so profuse that nine-tenths of the whole flows away into the Dala unused. The principal spring, that of St. Lawrence, comes up in an impetuous torrent, at a temperature of 120° Fahrenheit. The patients, most of whom are suffering from cutaneous or scrofulous disorders, commence by staying in the bath for an hour at a time. This is gradually increased till the bather remains immersed in saline tepid water for eight or nine hours daily. The tedium of spending so many hours alone would be intolerable. Hence the custom has originated of bathing together, and in public. Of course the strictest decorum is observed, and rules are laid down to regulate the dress and conduct of the bathers. The dresses are made of dark brown cloth. Conversation goes on freely. The baths are navigated by little tables of wood, at which the patients take their meals; ladies have their flowers or needlework, gentlemen their snuff-boxes or dominoes. The day is passed in breakfasting, chatting, reading, knitting, and playing at games of skill or chance; sometimes more boisterous sports are permitted, and I remember once looking on at a very vigorous game of Blind-man's-buff, played by bathers immersed to the chin in warm water.

The scenery of the Leukerbad Valley is impressive and beautiful under all conditions of light and atmospheric effect. But to be seen to perfection, like Melrose Abbey, "you should visit it by the pale moonlight." All scenery needs some specific condition of light and shade to bring out its highest beauty. The Lake of Thun should be seen in bright sunlight; the Lake of Lucerne with masses of mist and cloud floating to and fro, casting deep black shadows, and robing the mountains in mysterious gloom; the Valley of Chamouni is never so grand as at sunrise or sunset; the Gemmi should be seen from the gorge of the Dala in the light of the broad, full moon, as Cheever saw it: "The moon rose from behind the mountains, so that we had the hour and the scene of all others the most beautiful. No language can describe the extraordinary effect of the light falling on the mighty perpendicular crags and ridges of the Gemmi on the other side, while the village itself remained in darkness. It appeared as if the face of this mountain was gradually lighting up from an inward pale fire suffused in rich radiance over it, for it was hours before we could see the moon, though we could see her veil of soft light resting upon those gigantic, rock-ribbed regal barriers of nature.

"This beautiful night, after the moon was fully risen, I could not resist the temptation to walk down alone to that deep, wild, fir-clad gorge, through which the torrent of the Dala was thundering, that I might experience the full and uninterrupted impression of moonlight and solitude in so grand a scene. As I passed down from the village through the meadow slopes towards the black depths of the ravine, one or two persons were busied, though it was near midnight, silently mowing the grass. A beautiful grey mist, like the moonlight itself, lay upon the fields, and the sweep of the scythes through the wet grass was the only sound that rose upon the perfect stillness of the atmosphere, save the distant subterranean thunder of the falls of the Dala, buried in the depths of the chasm. Looking down into those depths amidst the din and fury of the waters, the sublimity of the impression is greatly heightened by the obscurity; and then looking upward along the forest of dark verdure that clothes the overhanging mountain, how still, how beautiful in the moonlight are those rising terraces of trees! They seem as if they, too, had an intelligent spirit, and were watching the night and enjoying its beauty."

From the foot of the Gemmi the gorge of the Dala leads us back into the Valley of the Rhone, some leagues lower down than where we last entered it at Visp and left it for the Æggisthorn.

THE MONT BLANC DISTRICT.

CRYSTAL SEEKERS ON MONT BLANC.

The Mont Blanc District.

THE TOUR OF MONT BLANC—THE COL DE BALME AND THE TÊTE NOIRE—CHAMOUNI—CONTAMINES—COL DU BONHOMME—THE RETURN OF THE WALDENSES—THE VALLEY OF THE ISÈRE—LAC DE COMBAL—COURMAYEUR—AOSTA—THE HOSPICE OF ST. BERNARD.

For those who do not aspire to emulate the exploits of the Alpine Club, the tour of Mont Blanc forms one of the most interesting and exciting excursions in Switzerland. Though it offers no difficulty which a fairly good pedestrian may not readily encounter, it leads the tourist amongst some of the sublimest and wildest scenery in the Alps. The beauty of the Val d'Aoste, the magnificence of the views of Mont Blanc from Courmayeur, the stern and savage grandeur of the Allée Blanche and Lac de Combal, and the combination of all these at Chamouni and the Tête Noire, leave little to be imagined or desired. The excursion may be easily completed within a week—in case of need, four or five days may suffice.

From Martigny to Chamouni the tourist by the Regular Swiss Round has to choose between the Col de Balme and the Valley of the Tête Noire.* The

* A preferable route to either is, in my judgment, to go from Martigny a couple of miles down the Rhone Valley, to Vernayaz, and cross the mountains, through the villages of Salvent and Finhaut. It is half an hour longer, and is little traversed, but the views are incomparably finer.

former is, as a whole, the less interesting of the two, but it has one view which is very grand. The pass of the Col de Balme is about 7000 feet high. It stretches right across the Valley of Chamouni, at the Martigny end, and from the summit, a view of Mont Blanc is gained,—perhaps the most perfect in Switzerland. You have, as it were, an observatory reared to a height of 7000 feet, to gaze upon a mountain of 16,000 feet. The Monarch stands revealed from base to summit surrounded by all his aiguilles and secondary heights, which stand like guards or courtiers around their king. The glaciers which clothe the sides of the mountains, the clouds which float over the valley or cling to the peaks, the broad valley itself, stretching right away to the Col de Voza, all add to the magnificence of the scene. The impressiveness of the view is yet further enhanced by its suddenness. During the ascent nothing is seen save the Col up which the traveller is toiling, till the summit is reached, when, as by magic, the stupendous view bursts upon him, and he feels and sees that

ENGLISH CHURCH AT CHAMOUNI.

> "Mont Blanc is the monarch of mountains;
> They crowned him long ago,
> On a throne of rocks, in a robe of clouds,
> With a diadem of snow."

MONTANVERT.

If the pass of the Tête Noire has no single view of such surpassing grandeur as that from the Col de Balme, it has a constant succession of softer beauties and milder glories, which, in the judgment of many, more than compensate for the loss. Unless the day be perfectly clear and bright, so as to secure the one grand view from the summit of the Col, there can be no doubt that the valley is preferable. Perhaps the most striking characteristic of this pass is its infinite variety and marvellous contrasts. Mountains lofty and precipitous, black jagged rocks, roaring torrents, dark gloomy ravines, solemn pine woods, between whose columnar trunks the path winds as through the aisles of a vast cathedral, yet withal an exhaustless abundance of exquisitely tinted flowers, delicate ferns, slopes on which the wild strawberry blushes and hides beneath her rich green leaves, and on all sides a profusion of verdure which softens down the ruggedness of the mountain forms, yet leaves their grandeur undiminished. What a concentration of all the elements of sublimity and beauty

VALLEY OF CHAMOUNI.

are here! What contrasts of light and shade, of form and colour, of softness and ruggedness! Here are vast heights above and vast depths below, villages hanging to the mountain sides, green pasturages, gloomy forests, châlets dotting the slopes, lovely meadows enamelled with flowers, dark immeasurable ravines, colossal overhanging walls and bastions of rock, domes of snow and naked peaks rising into the heavens!

Of Chamouni itself little need be said. Most persons have acquired some measure of familiarity with its scenery from the innumerable descriptions which have been given of it in poetry and prose, by speech, and pen and pencil. A few mean hovels, clustering round half a dozen huge hotels, set down amongst some of the grandest mountain scenery in the world, may suffice to describe this great centre of tourists of all nations. Every one has heard of the Montanvert, the Jardin, the Brévent, the Flegère, the Mer de Glace, the Grands Mulets. But the crowds of tourists can never vulgarise such scenes as these. They remain a marvel of grandeur and beauty, and a "joy for ever." It must, however, be admitted that there is something in the bustle and civilisation of Chamouni which takes off the edge of Alpine enjoyment. After a day in the mountains it is pleasant to descend into the valley, with its quiet inn and pleasant unpretending surroundings. Here you come back to a grand hotel with crowds of waiters and fine company, evening dress, Paris fashions, and London papers.

Two of the most popular excursions at Chamouni are to the Brévent and the Flegère: they are popular because the views are magnificent, and because the whole of the distance can be accomplished on mule-back. Both of these points are on the opposite side of the valley to the Mont Blanc range: the former is nearly in face of, although 7000 feet below, the summit; and the latter commands a splendid view up the Mer de Glace. From the latter the summit is distant just nine miles, and does not look more important than several inferior points; but immediately in face of the spectator a sharp snowy cone is seen—supported by ridges that diverge in all directions, which looks grander than anything else; this is the Aiguille Verte, a peak more than 2000 feet lower than the summit, but one that, from its commanding position, is seen to the greatest advantage in the Valley of Chamouni. Many men looked with longing eyes towards it, for, isolated as it is, it was known that it must give a view of unparalleled magnificence, and that a sight from it would make one understand the intricacies of the chain better than a month of gazing from inferior points. Many men tried to gain the summit, not only English, but French, and Swiss; they all met alike with failure, some beaten back by rocks too steep for human power, some by crevasses in the ice of a magnitude too great to be passed. Year by year went by, and the Aiguille Verte was still unascended, every failure provoking fresh attempts, and making men more anxious to do that in which others had failed to succeed. At length the task was accomplished by Mr. Edward Whymper, who gave a most interesting account of the ascent in the *Leisure Hour*, for August, 1866.

Continuing our tour round the base of Mont Blanc, the road leads down the Valley of Chamouni for about five miles, and then, turning to the left, mounts the Col de Vosa, which crosses the valley at the one end, as the Col de Balme crosses it at the other. The view, therefore, is exactly the counterpart to that already enjoyed on the way hither. Both look along the Valley of Chamouni; both command magnificent views of Mont Blanc; but, for many reasons, that

GATHERING EDELWEISS.

M

from the Col de Balme is the finer of the two. The summit of the Col is nearly 7000 feet high, yet, as Professor Forbes points out, erratic blocks are thickly strewn all around. How came they there? No torrent could have carried huge

THE AIGUILLE DE DRU, FROM NEAR THE MONTANVERT.

boulders of granite over such an elevation as this. He comes, therefore, to the conclusion—from which few will dissent—that here we have traces of glacial action; another proof, if any were needed, of the enormous extent to which the glaciers of Switzerland must have prevailed at some by-gone period.

The road then descends on the other side of the Col, passes the bright and cheerful Val de Montjoie, and allows a glimpse of the picturesque baths of St. Gervais, wedged in at the bottom of a deep ravine, the steep sides of which are densely covered with foliage and seamed with waterfalls. Contamines and the pilgrimage church of Notre Dame de la Gorge are soon reached. The church lies in a deep dell at the foot of Mont Joli. At the *fête* on the 15th August there is an immense concourse of the peasantry of the district. No better opportunity for seeing the costumes of the neighbouring valleys can be found. Contamines would seem to be one of the head-quarters of the adoration of the Virgin. The road-sides are thickly studded with chapels, shrines, images, and exhortations to worship her. In one place are these rude lines :

"Quand la mort fermera nos yeux
Accordez-nous, Reine des Cieux,
Le séjour des bienheureux :
Jésus et Maria ayez pitié de nous."

In an adjacent shrine is the blasphemous declaration :

"Qui invenerit Mariam
Inveniet Vitam."

On every side are declarations of indulgence to all who shall repeat a certain number of *aves* in her honour. How few of those who are taught thus to worship and trust in the Virgin have any true sense of the nature of faith in Jesus, or any knowledge of Him who is the Way, the Truth, and the Life!

THE COL DU BONHOMME.

After leaving Contamines the path assumes a wilder aspect; Nant Bourant, a frequent halting-place, is reached; and before long the Col du Bonhomme comes in sight. In fine weather and with a guide, there seems to be no special peril in crossing this dangerous pass,—the track appears so plain, the general direction so obvious. But let a fog form on the hills, or a snow-storm come on, and it is dreaded even by experienced guides. The wind drives the snow into fearful blinding eddies, all indications of the route are soon lost,

MONT BLANC AND THE VALLEY OF CHAMOUNI FROM SALLENCHES.

and the path, once strayed from, will with difficulty be found again. In the year 1830, two English gentlemen perished here. They were in the full vigour of early manhood. They left Nant Bourant in the morning for Chapiu, and were never again seen alive. Overtaken by a sudden snow-storm, they sank down and died on this desolate and dreary Col. Shortly before reaching the spot at which their bodies were found, a rude pile of stones is passed. Here, it is said,

ON THE MER DE GLACE.

a noble lady and her whole suite perished in a similar storm. Tradition has preserved the memory of the fact, but has lost the names of the sufferers. In passing the cairn the guides add a stone to the heap and request each traveller to do the same.*

* Perhaps it should be said that they used to do so. When I first crossed the Col, the custom was never omitted. Latterly it has been falling into desuetude. The jests and incredulity of the crowds of tourists have broken down the superstitious awe with which the spot was formerly regarded.

Reference has been repeatedly made to the great beauty of Alpine flowers, and to the fact that they flourish in the very drip of the glacier, lighting up the most dreary solitudes with their brilliant colours. This is nowhere more striking than around Lac de Combal, a lake more than 6000 feet above the level of the sea, surrounded by some of the wildest scenery of Switzerland, and fed by the great glaciers of the Miage and the Allée Blanche; yet even here "they make the wilderness and the solitary place glad, and the desert rejoices and blossoms as the rose."

> "Meek dwellers 'mid yon terror-stricken cliffs,
> With brows so pure, and incense-breathing lips,
> Whence are ye? Did some white-winged messenger
> On mercy's missions trust your timid germ
> To the cold cradle of eternal snows?
> Or, breathing on the callous icicles,
> Bid them with tear-drops nurse ye?
> * * * Tree nor shrub
> Dare that drear atmosphere; no polar pine
> Uprears a veteran front; yet there ye stand,
> Leaning your cheeks against the thick-ribbed ice,
> And looking up with brilliant eyes to Him
> Who bids you bloom unblanched amid the waste
> Of desolation."

As Courmayeur is approached, the landscape loses its bleak, sterile character, and the path winds through forests of ancient pines, whose branches are hung with long pendent streamers, like the Spanish moss of the American forests. The rocks are gay with brilliant many-coloured mosses and lichens. A rich profusion and infinite variety of ferns cluster in every nook and dingle; the hill-sides are carpeted with flowers, the magnificent glacier of La Brenva gleams purely white in the valley below; overhead, the huge cliffs of Mont Blanc rise like a mighty wall supporting a dome of snow, so bright, so pure, so ethereal, against the deep blue of the sky!

Courmayeur is nearly due south from Chamouni, the Monarch of mountains lying between them. Our tour has thus led us round the western flank of the Pennine Alps, and we have half completed the circuit of Mont Blanc. The distance from Courmayeur to Chamouni, in a direct line, is said to be only thirteen miles; but the ordinary tourist, who follows the line of valleys and climbs only the less difficult Cols round the base of the mountain, must take two or three days to accomplish the distance. The view of Mont Blanc from the Italian side is very different to that from the north. Excepting for the exquisite dome, so perfect in its outline, and so easy of identification from every point, it would scarcely be recognised as the same mountain. It is difficult to avoid a comparison of the two views, and almost equally difficult to award the preference to either. My own experience is that the present point of view always seems to be the noblest for the time being. But on the whole Chamouni bears away the palm. One night at Courmayeur, however, stands out in perpetual remembrance. We had come over the Col Seréna, and reached Morgex just at sunset. Twilight came down upon the valley, yet the mountain tops were all glowing in the sunlight. The lower peaks, one by one, sank into shadow as the gloom deepened around us. Still the higher summits were alight, burning like great altar-fires over the darkening earth. Soon, only the diadem of snow which crowns the highest point in Europe retained the heavenly radiance. For a few seconds a delicious rosy

COURMAYEUR.

blush overspread the pure crystalline dome, and then the light silently, almost imperceptibly, faded away, like life departing from the body, and only a cold, pure, ghostly whiteness remained. The lingering twilight faded into darkness. The stars shone out with intense brilliancy. Showers of meteors swept across the sky ; for it was the night of the August meteorolites. Suddenly a new gleam of light seemed mysteriously to rest on the highest summit. It was not sunlight —it was too purely white, too cold and chaste in tone and colour for the great king of day. It spread down the mountain sides, one peak after another caught the illumination, till at last the full moon rose over the Col behind us, and filled the valley with a flood of light.

The valley, from Courmayeur to Aosta—a distance of a little over twenty miles—is one succession of glorious views, each of which seems more impressive, more transcendently and indescribably beautiful than the last. Not without some show of reason is the village of Ivrogne said to be so named because you are "dazzled and drunk with beauty." One is ready to retract and apologise for the preference expressed for Chamouni over Courmayeur, and to say with Cheever, "I have seen Mont Blanc from all the best points of view, with every

VAL D'AOSTE.

advantage, so glorious that I then thought never could be presented such a juncture of elements in one picture of such unutterable sublimity and beauty. But, all taken together, no other view is to be compared for its magnificence with this in the Val d'Aoste." Still, notwithstanding the indescribable splendours of the Valley of Aosta, the judgment already expressed in favour of Chamouni is adhered to.

Aosta retains many traces of its Roman and imperial origin besides its name—a corruption of Augusta Prætoria. It claims, indeed, a much higher antiquity. Local antiquarians fix the date of its foundation at 406 years before the building of Rome by Romulus and Remus; that is to say, 1158 B.C.! It is certain that

THE GREAT ST. BERNARD.

it was the chief town of the Salassi, and that it was rebuilt by Augustus, who stationed here a detachment of 3000 men from his Prætorian Guard. Walls, bridges, gateways, an amphitheatre, and a triumphal arch, remain to illustrate the traditions which go back to the days of Roman occupation. St. Bernard, the apostle of the Alps, whose name is imperishably connected with the neighbouring mountain, pass, and monastery, lived here, and was archdeacon of the cathedral church of the city. Here, too, the illustrious Anselm was born—one of the very greatest evangelical theologians of the middle ages. He died Archbishop of Canterbury in 1109.

Aosta was for awhile the scene of the labours of Calvin, and a place of retreat from the persecutions of his enemies. But he was obliged, in the year 1541, to flee from this beautiful valley; and now in the city itself there is a stone cross, with an inscription at its base, to commemorate his departure, a curious testimony by the priests as to the power of this great man, and the dread with which his presence, his influence, and his labours were regarded among them. The inscription is in the following words: HANC CALVINI FUGÆ EREXIT ANNO MDXLI RELIGIONIS CONSTANTIA REPARAVIT ANNO MDCCXLI.

A curious story is still current, and firmly believed in the city and the valley, as to the cause of Calvin's flight. It is said that he had promised the people, as a sign of the truth of his teaching, to raise a dead man to life; that he made the attempt and failed, and that the whole city was so enraged against him that he had to flee at midnight, or rather at eleven o'clock, across the Grand St. Bernard, to save himself from destruction. As a proof of this legend, the inhabitants of Aosta, to commemorate the event, have ever since made the hour of eleven their midday and midnight, so that they dine at eleven instead of twelve, and consider eleven as noon. A far truer and worthier relic of Calvin's presence and labours in Aosta is to be found in the fact that a few Protestant families have held their ground ever since, true to the faith of their fathers, amidst obloquy and persecution.

Nowhere are goitre and cretinism more prevalent than in this beautiful valley. The peasantry are beyond description squalid and filthy; scarcely a well-dressed or decent-looking person is to be met. All bear the marks of poverty, disease, and wretchedness. Heber's familiar line applies with terrible truth to the inhabitants of this lovely region—"Every prospect pleases, and only man is vile."

The next stage in the tour of Mont Blanc is from Aosta to the Pass and Monastery of St. Bernard. There is comparatively little to interest in the early part of the journey. Cars convey the tourist to St. Remy, and mules the rest of the way. The scenery, though wild and stern, is not particularly striking. But the first view of the famous monastery, standing in lonely grandeur at the head of the pass, is a sight not to be soon forgotten. The lights streaming through the windows afford a welcome sight even to the summer tourist overtaken by nightfall as he toils up the ascent. What must it be to the unhappy peasant compelled to cross amidst the storms of winter! Well-deserved is the tribute paid by Rogers to

"That door which, even as self-opened, moves,
To them that knock, and nightly sends abroad
Ministering spirits. . . .
Long could I have stood
With a religious awe contemplating
That house, the highest in the ancient world,
And destined to perform from age to age
The noblest service, welcoming as guests
All of all nations and of every faith;
A temple sacred to humanity!"

The historical associations of the pass go back to a remote antiquity. The Celtic tribes who occupied the surrounding regions at the dawn of European history reared, on the plateau, a cairn to their god Penn—a deity to whom the highest mountain-tops were deemed sacred, and whose memory lingers in our own topography in such names as Ben Lomond and Ben Nevis, Pendennis and Penmaenmawr. When the victorious legions of Rome had subdued the Veragri and Salassi, whose territories extended to the summit of the pass, the rude pile of stones sacred to the god Penn was changed into a temple to Jupiter Penninus. Of this temple some fragments yet remain. Tablets and votive offerings placed in the temple and on the altar by travellers, in grateful acknowledgment of escape from the perils of the pass, have been dug up. It is from the god Penn in his Latinised form Penninus that the Pennine Alps take their name. Mont Joux is likewise a corruption of Mons Jovis. A hospice was founded on the summit of the pass in the days of the Carlovingians, and it took its name of Bernard from one or other of two princes of that family, each of whom led an army by this route into Italy. The present hospice was founded by St. Bernard, to whom reference has already been made, and who must not be confounded with the better known Bernard of Clairvaux. He may have been attracted by the coincidence of its name with his own. It had been ravaged and devastated by the Saracens, whose traces we have met with at the other end of the Pennine chain. He restored it, and dedicated it to his favourite Saint, Nicolas de Myre. But his own name has superseded all others, and the hospice is known to the whole civilized world as that of St. Bernard. In the stormy times which followed, the monastery was often plundered by bands of marauders, and the name of our Canute appears amongst those who complained to the pope and the emperor of the insecurity of the pass. In the long intricate feuds between Germany and Italy, pope and emperor, Guelph and Ghibelline, we constantly read of the one party or the other making a foray or marching an army across the Great St. Bernard. But, in the words of Milton, these obscure conflicts have little more interest than those of the kites and the crows. In modern times the passage of the St. Bernard by Napoleon, at the head of 80,000 men, with a proportionate number of cannon, is familiar to all readers.

DOGS OF ST. BERNARD.

To many visitors, the scene of greatest interest at the hospice is the morgue, or building where the dead bodies of travellers are deposited. There they are some of them as when the breath of life departed, and the death-angel, with frost and snow, fixed them for ages. The floor is strewn with nameless skulls and bones and human dust heaped in confusion. But around the walls are groups of sufferers in the very position in which they were found; rigid as marble, and in this keen dry air, by the preserving element of an eternal frost, almost as uncrumbling. There is a mother and her child, a most affecting image of suffering and love. The face of the little one remains pressed to the mother's bosom, only the back part of the skull being visible, the body enfolded in her careful arms, careful in vain, affectionate in vain, to shield her offspring from the wrath of the tempest. The snow fell fast and thick, and the hurricane wound both up in one white shroud and buried them. There is a tall strong man standing alone, the face dried and black, the white teeth firmly set and closed, grinning from fleshless jaws—an awful spectacle. The face seems to look at you from the recesses of the sepulchre, as if it would tell you the story of a fearful death-struggle in the storm. There are other groups, more indistinct, but these two are at once imprinted on the tablets of the memory, and the whole of these dried and frozen remnants of humanity are a terrific demonstration of the fearfulness of this mountain-pass, when the elements, let loose in fury, encounter the unhappy traveller.

Leaving the hospice, a rough but not very steep path leads down to St. Pierre, or Liddes. From hence to Martigny, a distance of about twenty miles, there is a good road all the way, and the tour of Mont Blanc is ignominiously brought to a conclusion in an omnibus which runs between Martigny and St. Pierre daily.

WESTERN SWITZERLAND.

WHICH IS THE WAY?

WESTERN SWITZERLAND.

THE RHONE VALLEY AND THE CANTON DE VAUD—CHAMPERY—THE VAL ORMONT—SEPEY—THE CREUX DES CHAMPS—ROUGEMONT—LAKE LEMAN—CASTLE OF CHILLON—GENEVA—CALVIN AND FAREL—MADAME GUYON—FELIX NEFF—LAUSANNE—THE JURA—NEUFCHATEL—GAP.

THE Rhone, after flowing in a westerly direction from its birthplace in the glacier, suddenly turns to the northward on reaching Martigny, and runs at a right angle to its former course till it enters the Lake of Geneva. Our route lies along this part of its banks. A railway traverses the valley, and as the scenery is not very striking, little is lost by adopting the speedier mode of transit, at least as far as Bex. Near Martigny a very fine cascade is passed—the Pissevache—but it can be seen quite well from the road, and the tourist is probably, by this time, satiated with waterfalls. On leaving Martigny the road continues for some time in the Canton Valais—a Catholic canton—and the squalor, misery, and poverty apparent in other parts of the Rhone Valley meet the eye at every turn. At St. Maurice the Protestant Canton de Vaud is reached, and, at once all is changed. Thriving homesteads, well-kept farms, smiling villages attest the altered habits of the people.

At St. Maurice the River Rhone is suddenly contracted within a narrow gorge, and is crossed by a bridge of a single arch. This makes it an important strategic point. On more than one occasion the Swiss have availed themselves of it in defence of their liberty. It was formerly closed by a gate, now replaced by a fort. To this Rogers makes allusion:

"Journeying upward by the Rhone,
That there came down a torrent from the Alps,
I entered where a key unlocks a kingdom:
The road, the river, as they wind along
Filling the mountain-pass."

Through the Rhone Valley is a beaten track, crowded, during the season, with visitors from every nationality in Europe; there are, nevertheless, within easy distance on either side, spots of transcendent beauty and grandeur, scarcely visited, and little known. Tourists are for the most part gregarious. They travel in crowds. The consequence is that certain places, which happen to be the fashion, are filled to overflowing, whilst others, in no respect inferior, are passed without a pause. Until recently very few of all the thousands who annually pour along the Rhone Valley ever stopped at Bex or Monthey to visit Champery. Yet there are few more charming villages in Switzerland. The views of the Dent du Midi and the Val d'Illiez are of surpassing grandeur and beauty.

ST. MAURICE.

Equally beautiful, but even less visited, is the Val Ormont, on the opposite side the Rhone Valley. The road turns off at Aigle. In about an hour Sepey is reached, a quaint straggling village composed entirely of wooden châlets, which, with their overhanging roofs, their covered galleries, and their carved gables, have a very picturesque effect. Many of the gable-fronts are inscribed with texts of Scripture, verses, and prayers, carved and painted in bright colours. A homely village inn receives guests *en pension* at a very moderate rate. A writer in the *Leisure Hour* describes some days spent here a few years ago:—"Our view from the rude wooden gallery, which served as our *salon*, was one which stamped itself upon the heart and mind with a vividness never to be effaced. The peaceful

DENT DU MIDI.

pastoral foreground, with its swelling mounds of verdure, its bright rapid stream, its quaint châlets, its cattle, with their bells ringing out clearly in the evening air, and the peasantry lingering on their homeward way in cheerful conversation—the whole scene, so full of homely yet picturesque beauty, standing out in bold relief against a panoramic range of Alps—'mountain upon mountain piled,' with their snowy peaks, dark fantastic crags, sombre forests, and gleaming waterfalls; such were the objects on which we sat gazing until the shadows of evening fell upon the landscape, imparting to it a stiller and more solemn beauty.

"Next morning came the day of rest; and we were glad to have the opportunity of passing it among those who are regarded in Switzerland as the truest and most fervent professors of the Protestant faith. It was communion Sunday. Divine service was not to begin until ten o'clock, but it was still early in the morning when we observed groups of people approaching from all sides of the country. Along every mountain path and through every opening gorge might be seen, advancing at intervals, some family of peasants: the aged white-haired man resting on his staff, and the youth, whose lofty brow and upright manliness spoke alike of firmness and of daring; the staid matron, and the young girl just emerging from childhood—all were hastening to the

AT SEPEY.

house of God. The many paths thus dotted with peasantry all converged to the village of Sepey, from whence an upland road led to the village church, which lay at about a quarter of a mile distant. We mingled with the ascending throng, and, on emerging from a pretty copse-like wood, saw before us the dark grey tower of the church, which stood on the sloping brow of the hill, surrounded by the silent resting-places of the dead. No sculptured tombs were there, but many nameless green mounds, and a few distinguished by a wooden head-rail, whereon were carved the name and age of the deceased.

"Divided from the churchyard only by a narrow rudely-paved road stood the parsonage, a large wooden châlet of the same class as the superior ones in the village. It was placed between a small paddock and a garden, wherein flowers and vegetables grew together in friendly neighbourhood. A few old men sat talking on a long wooden bench outside the roofed gateway of the churchyard; but most of the congregation were hastening within the walls of the church. We followed them, and found the building—a tolerably large one—already thronged with people.

"Several minutes elapsed before the beginning of the service, so we had full leisure to contemplate the scene around us. At the right side of the church stood, close to the wall, an elevated pulpit, beside which was placed an hour-glass—the relic, doubtless, of those olden times when sermons were wont to be meted out in their several parts by the falling sands of time. Beneath it, in the centre of the church, stood the communion table; and near it were the seats for the elders, fashioned like stalls, while the other seats were merely open benches with backs like those in many of our modern English churches. All the seats were placed so as to face the communion table and the pulpit. Every available spot was closely crowded with people, the men and women being seated at different sides of the church: but the men were in great majority on this occasion, for neither in the chancel nor galleries was a woman to be seen.

"Perfect stillness pervaded this dense mass of human beings. A primitive, noble-looking race they were: the men, earnest, thoughtful, intelligent, tall in stature, and resolute in aspect, looking as if they could not only dare, but also suffer for their faith. Their clothing was of dark homespun cloth, cut in long square-fashioned habiliments. The women, young and old, were clad in dark dresses, over which were carefully folded and pinned large silk handkerchiefs or shawls of green or dark blue silk, bordered with some gayer colour, while on their heads they all wore *toques* of black silk or velvet, trimmed with broad frills of black lace. Not a single bonneted female was to be seen in the congregation, except the pastor's wife and sister, and the ladies of our own party.

"A sad-looking clerk, with a black garment hanging down from his shoulders behind, having entered the pulpit, read aloud a chapter in the Bible, and then gave out a hymn, which was sung with hearty vehemence by the whole congregation. This concluded, the pastor, a grave, intelligent young man, ascended the pulpit, and repeated with solemnity and fervour some excellent prayers out of the Swiss-Vaudois prayer-book. The congregation stood up, but seemed rather to listen to than to unite in their pastor's prayers. Another hymn followed; and then the pastor opened his Bible and gave out as his text that solemn and heart-stirring declaration of the God of Israel to his rebellious people: 'As I live, saith the Lord God, I have no pleasure in the death of the wicked; but that the wicked turn from his way and live; turn ye, turn ye from your evil ways; for why will ye die, O house of Israel?' After comparing God's yearning over sinners to the feelings of a tender mother, who seeth her children advancing blindly or recklessly to the edge of a precipice, entreats them to turn away from it, the pastor besought his hearers not to *speculate* about the mystery of God's willing our salvation, and yet that we must will it too. 'We are,' said he, 'in a house in flames. The way is open to escape. God would save you. Do not wait to reason; but enter at once into the plan of His boundless mercy and compassion, as revealed in Christ

Jesus.' Every eye was riveted on the preacher as he expounded a message so full of awe and of mercy. During the sermon, he gave utterance to two or three brief petitions for the people, and it was curious to see how instantaneously every head was uncovered (for many had put on their hats at the conclusion of the devotions), and how rapidly the hats were replaced as soon as the pastor's 'Amen' had been uttered. It seemed as though, in proportion to their independence of outward things, they were careful to express their reverence towards a prayer-hearing and prayer-answering God.

"The sermon over, the pastor repeated the Lord's Prayer, the Apostles' Creed, and the Ten Commandments, together with the brief summary of them given by our Lord in the New Testament. He then read aloud, in a most earnest, impressive manner, an address to the people on the origin and meaning of the Lord's Supper, with a solemn excommunication of all those who through wilful sin or unbelief were not worthy to partake of it. At the conclusion of the address the pastor sat down. There was a deep silence in the church.

"We expected, after so solemn a warning, that a large proportion of the congregation would depart; but all remained still and motionless in their places. After a few moments' pause the pastor left the pulpit, and placing himself at one end of the communion table, blessed the bread and wine which were placed before him. He then called three elders, grave, noble-looking old men, bearing in their hands a flagon and two chalices, and gave them authority to present the wine to the communicants. He himself remained standing at the north end of the table, with a large salver in his hand, piled up with bread; while at the other end stood the three elders, two of them holding the chalices, and the other a flagon of wine. A few words were then spoken by the pastor, exhorting the people to listen reverently to God's Word; whereon the clerk resumed his place in the pulpit and read aloud in a monotonous tone several of the concluding chapters of St. John's Gospel, with a commentary on the same, which, alternating with the singing of hymns, continued during the celebration of the communion.

"Meanwhile the men began to move from their places, and advancing in close but orderly procession, approached the pastor, who handed to each a bit of bread, which was received with a bow; and passing on in front of the table, the wine was presented to them by the two elders. The communicants returned to their seats by another way, so that during the space of two hours or thereabouts there was a ceaseless flow of people, moving on rapidly, yet gravely, throughout the church. The pastor stood perfectly silent the whole time; but his eye was fixed steadily on each communicant as he approached, and the expression of that eye often bespoke sorrow or reproof more eloquently than if his lips had uttered those feelings aloud. When all the men in the church had received the communion, then the women approached in like order. On their being reseated in their places, the pastor once more ascended the pulpit, and concluded the service by a prayer and an address to the communicants on the duties and responsibilities of those who had partaken of that holy ordinance."

About three hours from Sepey, up a rough, but not steep ascent, the tourist reaches the Plan des Isles, and the Creux des Champs—a spot of perfect enchantment, combining all the elements of beauty and grandeur. The valleys from hence to Thun are famous throughout Switzerland for their exceeding richness and fertility. Their cheese and butter are considered the best in the land. Here, too, the best riflemen in the Confederation are said to live. It is a Protestant, liberty-loving, thriving district. The green slopes are dotted with innumerable châlets. From the Alps above, and the meadows below, the musical tones of the cattle-bells are heard. The hills on the northern side, though their summits are easily accessible, command grand panoramic views, extending over the Jura, the chain of the Bernese Oberland, the Pennine Alps from Monte Rosa to Mont Blanc, the wild chaos of peaks that stand around the Dent du Midi and the Lake of Geneva. I scarcely know any ascent so easy, rewarded by a panorama so complete, a view so grand. The valley is bounded on the other side by a range of mountains, rising to a height of 11,000 feet, mantled with ice and snow. It is the Creux des Champs, however, which gives its peculiar character to this part of the valley. The Creux is an immense amphitheatre or *cirque*, like those of the Pyrenees, only far grander and vaster, penetrating for a couple of miles into the side of the mountain. Its precipitous walls are surmounted by glaciers and snow-fields. Innumerable cascades fall from the glaciers down the rocky sides of the amphitheatre, and form a roaring torrent, which thunders grandly through the pine-woods, and then subsides into calm as it reaches the rich green meadows.

OBERLAND CHÂLET.

Amongst many delightful seasons spent in the Ormont-dessus, one Sunday stands out with great prominence. It was indeed "a day much to be remembered." In the morning we walked "with the voice of joy and praise" to the little church, which lay a couple of miles down the valley. It seemed impossible not to praise God as we went. The day was perfect. The path lay through meadows of an intense green, bright with a thousand flowers, over which clouds of butterflies hovered and sported. At our feet the infant Eau Noir babbled noisily. Less than an hour ago its waters, now hurrying past us, had leaped from the heart of the Sans Fleuron glacier, had plunged headlong, a thousand feet, down the precipitous walls of the Creux des Champs, had rushed, as though terror-stricken, through the dark gloomy depths of the pine forest which fills up the *cirque*, and now bursting out into brilliant sunlight and rambling on between green and flowery banks seemed to be fairly singing for joy,

> "Making sweet music to each little sedge,
> As forth it hasted on its pilgrimage."

Above us frowned huge masses of naked rock crowned with eternal snow. Groups of worshippers dressed in the *bizarre* yet picturesque costume of the district were emerging from every châlet, or wending their way down the mountain sides.

Approaching the church, we found it standing in the centre of the pastor's garden. Flowers were trained up the porch and peeped in at the open windows. The fragrance of new-mown hay came floating on the breeze. The soft and distant music of cattle-bells, the twittering of birds, and the murmuring of the stream, were the only audible sounds. As the congregation assembled we were greatly struck by their devoutness of manner. Subsequent conversation with many of them showed that manner was, in this case, but the outward expression of deep religious feeling. One custom, which we observed here for the first time, greatly pleased us. The congregation, as they entered the church, reverently paused for a few seconds on the threshold, bowed their heads, crossed their arms upon their breasts, and silently repeated a short prayer. Then, but not till then, they took their places on the open benches with which the church was seated.

The service—that of the *Eglise libre* of the Canton de Vaud—was plain, simple, and impressive. The sermon was from Rom. iii. 27: "Where is boasting then? It is excluded. By what law? of works? Nay; but by the law of faith." It was an earnest, evangelical discourse. The point specially insisted upon was that salvation by works, even if it were possible, could only produce pride and selfishness in man, and rob God of His glory; whilst salvation by faith humbles man, and glorifies God. Some of our party thought the discourse altogether too doctrinal and abstruse for the congregation. This, however, did not seem to be the opinion of the hearers themselves. They eagerly listened to every word, and by their subsequent remarks showed that their minds, quickened and energized by familiarity with the sublime truths of the gospel, were capable of grappling with the great themes under discussion.

At the close of the service it was announced that a meeting for worship would be held in the evening, in the pine forest behind the mill. To this service we went. The place of meeting was amongst the pines which fill the vast amphitheatre of the Creux des Champs. A nobler temple can hardly be imagined. Around us arose the columnar trunks of mighty trees like the pillars of a vast cathedral. The branches overhead formed a roof whose immense height and delicate tracery left all Gothic architecture at a hopeless distance. The slanting rays of the evening sun came flickering down upon us as in showers of golden rain. Through glades and openings in the forest the vast glaciers and snow-fields of the Diablerets were visible. Overhead towered the Oldenhorn

CREUX DES CHAMPS.

and his brother giants to the height of 10,000 or 11,000 feet. These mighty peaks and aiguilles, cut so sharp and clear against the evening sky, seemed to rise and mingle with the stars, which began to peep out through the fading light. The roar of innumerable cataracts plunging down the mountain sides, from the glaciers above, kept up a solemn sound like distant thunder.

A congregation of about two hundred persons assembled. They sat upon tufts of moss, trunks of fallen trees, stumps and roots left in the ground by the woodmen; a few stood in groups where they could hear most advantageously. No painter could have grouped them with more pictorial effect. All ages were there—old men and women, their faces furrowed and wrinkled and weatherworn, herdsmen and hunters from the Alps above us, mothers with infants on their knees or at their breasts, young men and maidens walking side by side, and little children who whiled away the interval by seeking strawberries and bilberries. At length the service began. Grandly rose the psalm, the waterfalls thundering a ceaseless bass. The officiating minister—a venerable white-haired man—was an evangelist employed to itinerate amongst the scattered châlets and hamlets in the mountains and hold services with the herdsmen. An English minister who happened to be in our party was requested to take part in the service and speak to the people. This he did; and the address, though simple and unstudied, was listened to with tears. He spoke of the unity of all believers in Christ, that in Him "there is neither Greek nor Jew, barbarian, Scythian, bond or free;" but all are one in the Saviour. "We have never met before," he said, "we shall probably never meet again on earth. We are strangers to each other. Our speech, our manners, our modes of life are utterly unlike. And yet, my brothers, my sisters, I claim you as members of one family, children of one Father, brethren of one Elder Brother, to live with us for ever in the same happy home, our Father's house whither Jesus has gone to prepare a place for us." Then adverting to the distant journey we had undertaken in order to gaze upon the magnificent scenery around us, he spoke of the pilgrimage to a yet more beautiful and glorious world to which Christ invites us, and implored those who had not yet begun to tread that path and seek that better country to do so without delay.

In no part of Switzerland can the simple life of the peasantry be better seen than here. The extortion and the begging which annoy the traveller in the beaten track of tourists are rarely encountered. Unchanged by foreign influence, uncontaminated by the servile spirit which springs up in the train of visitors, they here display their better qualities.

> "A true and noble-hearted race are they
> Who dwell in Ormond's upland vale,
> Free as the chamois on their mountain's side!
> Firm as the rocks which hem their valley in!
> They keep the faith for which their father's fought:
> They fear their God, nor fear they aught beside."

Miss Whately, a recent resident in one of the châlet-pensions of the district, thus records the impression they produced upon her mind, and the result of her efforts for their spiritual benefit:

"Ours is just such a pretty, fanciful Swiss cottage as pictures and stories had made us familiar with—looking out on a glorious view. Behind the house rise green mountain-heights, with views of higher Alps beyond. Opposite our windows is the bare and rocky summit of the Rubli, its sides clothed with pine forests or green slopes studded with châlets. Through the middle of the valley, the rapid River Sarine, which descends from the glaciers of the Valaisian Alps, winds through a deep rocky glen, bordered with pine forests, whose banks are green with the richest moss, and luxuriant in ferns, wild flowers, and mountain berries.

"Such is our new mountain home. Our life in it is truly primitive: we keep early hours, as all do here, the principal meal being taken at a little past noon;

THE PENSION-CHÂLET, ROUGEMONT.

and all the arrangements of the house are sufficiently simple: one might imagine oneself in a perpetual picnic. But if the little refinements and elegancies of town life are wanting, we have luxuries which elsewhere would be unattainable—the most abundant and excellent supply of all dairy products, especially the richest cream; alpine strawberries and raspberries in profusion, and provisions in general cheap and good. Our hosts are specimens of the well-to-do class in these mountains, owners of two or three châlets in different parts of the neighbouring Alps, and a large herd of cattle—the chief wealth of the country. At these upper châlets, or *fruiteries*, the making of the famous Gruyère cheeses, and others of a more homely kind, forms the staple industry. The master keeps several men at work, and himself goes up part of every week to one châlet or another. When the lower pastures have been sufficiently consumed, the cattle are led to a higher. There is, therefore, a perpetual movement in the summer season, from pasture to pasture; and even in the middle of the night we are sometimes roused by the ringing of cattle-bells, which announce the progress of a herd to or from its châlet. These herds are generally between twenty and thirty in number, and frequently from eighty to a hundred; the cows very large, far more so than any one sees at home, very handsome, tame, and intelligent. But a walk through the valley will give the best idea of this pastoral life.

GIRLS LEADING CATTLE TO THE MOUNTAINS.

"Early in the morning or late in the evening we generally see one or more horses descending from the mountains, laden with a curious wooden machine for holding cheeses, their bells, adorned with coloured tassels, ringing as they go. As we walk through the village, a man or boy, carrying a similar machine on his back, or wheeling one in a sort of barrow, often meets us. The women are much employed in field-work, and as we pass the grassy slopes we see them in their wide, shady hats, busily making hay, sometimes on the sides of hills so steep that to keep one's balance would require some ingenuity; lives have sometimes been lost from haymakers slipping down these precipitous slopes. As we pass along every few

IN THE CANTON DE VAUD.

yards brings us to a fresh spring of clear, sparkling water, generally carried through a rough channel, made of a hollow tree, into a trough with a spout above it.

"It would be endless and tedious to describe the variety of walks and excursions around our valley; every day we discovered new beauties. The abundance of wild flowers surpassed every expectation we had formed; they were of every size and shape, and comprised many kinds that we had never seen before. Our party made two excursions to the higher châlets on the upland pastures, above the pine forests, where the slopes of short grass, mingled with wild thyme and delicate small flowers, afford grazing for the large herds of cattle; the mountain breeze is refreshing in the hottest days, and the eye can wander to a perfect panorama of distant Alps.

"We early felt it was a responsibility laid on us, as residents for a considerable time in the valley, to endeavour to do what we could in promoting the

MUSTERING FOR THE SCHOOL TREAT.

higher welfare of those around us. Very little is needed in this canton as to temporal relief; the inhabitants, for the most part, live in comfort, and what would be considered affluence among our working classes; occasional distress is assisted by the commune; but it cannot be said that similar provision is made for spiritual wants. The national church in the Canton de Vaud is in a sad lifeless state. The government regulations for some years past have been such as to drive the larger part of the earnest and devoted clergy out of the church.

"Every alternate Sunday a meeting of the *Eglise libre* is held in a châlet a little way above us, and these meetings were all we could desire. The pastor of Chateau d'Oex and his assistant come by turns to preside at this little meeting, and the expositions and prayers are full of spirituality, unction, and force. There is also a little meeting every Sunday, held by some simple, quiet, earnest

Christians belonging to a peculiar sect, but without any of the sectarianism of spirit often found in such communities.

"Among the simple mountaineers of Rougemont and Chateau d'Oex we met with several who seemed to possess deep and vital piety, and also much intelligence; and there was a very general readiness to receive tracts and religious books. But our most interesting undertaking was the formation of a Sunday afternoon school. This work had been commenced by some English friends, who had preceded us in our abode here. They had been led almost by an accidental circumstance to open the school, and had continued it through a whole winter with success. No such institution existed in the place, the religious instruction of the children being confined to a public catechising in the church on Sunday mornings. On the second Sunday of our arrival a goodly number of children of all ages were seen before our door, many of them bringing little offerings of flowers and berries, the flowers beautifully and tastefully arranged in bouquets and wreaths. We found they had been begging for contributions from all the gardens round. The numbers were too great for our little *salle à manger*, so they were distributed between that, the balcony, and a large barn at the back of the house. We found our pupils very intelligent, and, with scarce an exception, docile, well-behaved, and anxious to learn. It was really a cheering task to teach them, and the interest they showed could not be mistaken. The mothers often came into the barn to listen to the teaching, and we had several encouraging proofs that a real desire to learn had been awakened. For instance: one evening, as we were passing through the village, we observed several of our pupils forming a little group at a cottage door, and evidently intent on something they were reading. We found they were in the habit of forming themselves into a little kind of evening school, quite of their own accord, to study the text of the week and to read their tracts. By the elder people we were continually stopped and asked for books. A woman one day accosted us in going up the mountain behind our house, and asked if we had any of the 'feuilles religieuses' we had been giving the children, she liked them so much. Fortunately I was provided with some, and could gratify her. Another day I met a girl with one of the heavy, cornucopia-like baskets on her back which they all use here: she came to meet me and asked me for a book. Two of her sisters came to the Sunday-school, she said, and could we give her or sell her one of the little books we had given or lent them? I had none about me, but told her if she would come home with me I would get her some. She willingly laid down her burden, and walked all the way back with me, full half a mile, to procure the wished-for books. She had been afraid to come to the school herself, but on my persuasion she promised to come and bring three others with her, but she was obliged to go up to the mountains, and could not follow up her intention.

"In Canton de Vaud reading is universal; it is penal in the canton for a father to allow his child to grow up without education, and inspectors go round from time to time to ascertain if the children can read and write. Village schools are universal, and accordingly it is rare to find a child of twelve years old who cannot both read and write. Bibles or Testaments are found in most of the houses."

Returning to the Rhone Valley, the railway takes us very speedily to Villeneuve, and here we reach the Lake of Geneva. It is the largest lake in Switzerland, and, in some respects, the most beautiful. It has nothing of the grandeur and sublimity of the lakes of Lucerne and Thun. It wants the marvellous richness and glow of colour which the Italian lakes possess; but for bright, cheerful, *riant* beauty it is pre-eminent amongst those of Switzerland. The cantos in *Childe Harold* describing the lake in calm and storm are familiar, but

THE LAKE AND CITY OF GENEVA.

cannot be omitted here. Very touching is the tone of sadness, the deep craving for peace which the aspect of the lake excites in the mind of the unhappy poet:

"Clear placid Leman! thy contrasted lake,
With the wild world I dwell in, is a thing
Which warns me, with its stillness, to forsake
Earth's troubled waters for a purer spring.
This quiet sail is as a noiseless wing
To waft me from distraction; once I loved
Torn ocean's roar, but thy soft murmuring
Sounds sweet as if a Sister's voice reproved,
That I with stern delights should e'er have been so moved.

It is the hush of night, and all between
Thy margin and the mountains, dusk, yet clear,
Mellowed and mingling, yet distinctly seen,
Save darkened Jura, whose capt heights appear

Precipitously steep; and drawing near,
There breathes a living fragrance from the shore,
Of flowers yet fresh with childhood; on the ear
Drops the light drip of the suspended oar,
Or chirps the grasshopper one good-night carol more;

He is an evening reveller, who makes
His life an infancy, and sings his fill;
At intervals, some bird from out the brakes
Starts into voice a moment, then is still.
There seems a floating whisper on the hill,
But that is fancy,—for the starlight dews
All silently their tears of love instil,
Weeping themselves away, till they infuse
Deep into Nature's breast the spirit of her hues. . . .

The sky is changed!—and such a change! O night,
And storm, and darkness, ye are wondrous strong,
Yet lovely in your strength, as is the light
Of a dark eye in woman! Far along,
From peak to peak, the rattling crags among
Leaps the live thunder! Not from one lone cloud,
But every mountain now hath found a tongue,
And Jura answers, through her misty shroud,
Back to the joyous Alps, who call to her aloud! . . . .

Now, where the swift Rhone cleaves his way between
Heights which appear as lovers who have parted
In hate, whose mining depths so intervene
That they can meet no more, though broken-hearted!
Though in their souls, which thus each other thwarted,
Love was the very root of the fond rage
Which blighted their life's bloom, and then departed:
Itself expired, but leaving them an age
Of years all winters,—war within themselves to wage.

Now, where the quick Rhone thus hath cleft his way,
The mightiest of the storms hath ta'en his stand:
For here, not one, but many, make their play,
And fling their thunder-bolts from hand to hand,
Flashing and cast around: of all the band,
The brightest through these parted hills hath forked
His lightnings,—as if he did understand,
That in such gaps as desolation worked,
There the hot shaft should blast whatever therein lurked.

Sky, mountains, river, winds, lake, lightnings! ye,
With night, and clouds, and thunder, and a soul
To make these felt and feeling, well may be
Things that have made me watchful; the far roll
Of your departing voices, is the knoll
Of what in me is sleepless,—if I rest.
But where of ye, O tempests! is the goal?
Are ye like those within the human breast?
Or do ye find, at length, like eagles, some high nest?"

E. WHYMPER, LONDON. BY HODSON'S CHROMOGRAPHIC PROCESS.

MONT BLANC from above MORGES.

Few objects in Switzerland are more familiar, [illegible] hackneyed, than the Castle of Chillon. [illegible] been painted by the artist and described by the [illegible] a striking object; it is neither massive nor very [illegible] site is greatly diminished by the railway which runs close to it. But the sad story of Bonnivard, the prisoner of Chillon, and the innumerable poetical associations which cluster around the antique walls, will make it an object of deep and perpetual interest. The interior of the castle well repays a visit. The torture chamber, the beam on

which criminals were hung; the *oubliette*, [illegible] from which was through a trap-door in the floor [illegible] worn by the pacing to and fro of the prisoners, are all [illegible] the place. The castle is now used by the canton as a [illegible]

As the end of the lake is approached [illegible] and the scenery suffers in [illegible] advantage, that it allows of [illegible] Nothing can be more exquisitely [illegible] waters of the lake to the [illegible] of evening. The flush of rosy light [illegible] is quite unearthly in its effect. [illegible] in reflection. Here, too, the mountain [illegible] a mighty mirror.

Geneva lies at the [illegible] Most visitors are [illegible] the picturesque irregularity and air of [illegible] which characte

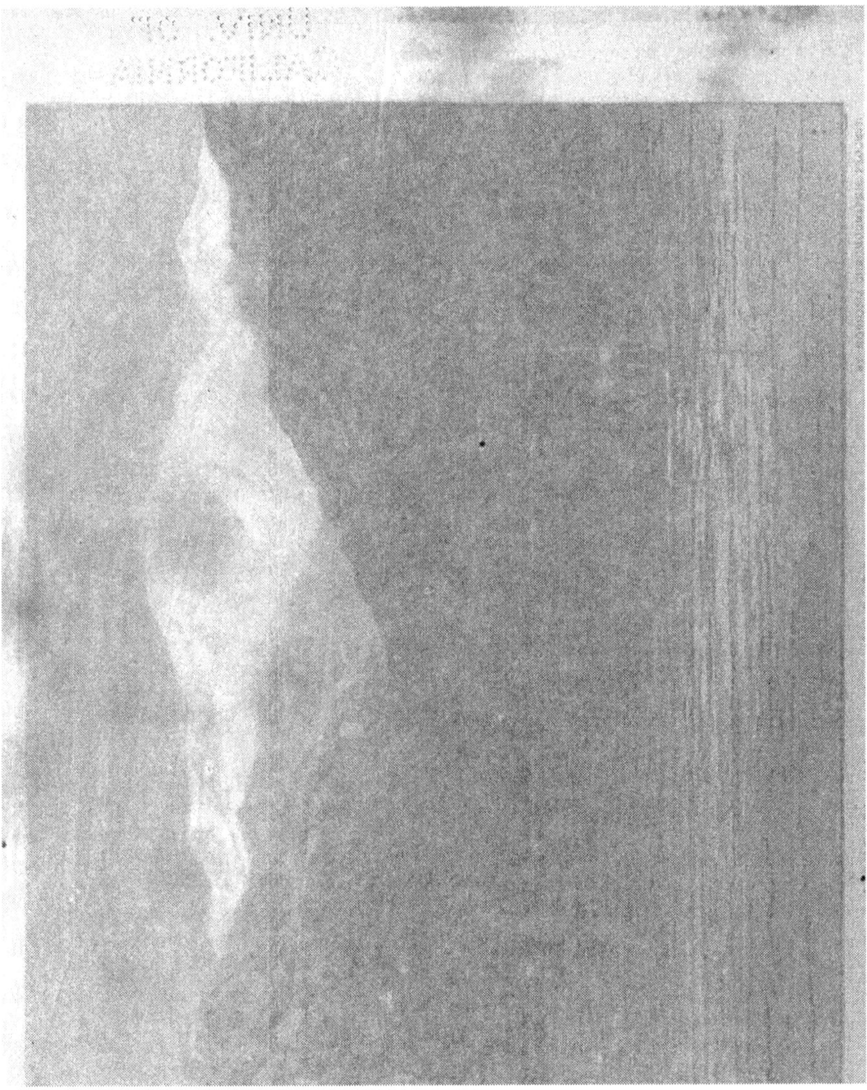

Few objects in Switzerland are more familiar, it might almost be said, hackneyed, than the Castle of Chillon, on the edge of the lake; so often has it been painted by the artist and described by the poet. The castle itself is not a striking object; it is neither massive nor very picturesque; the beauty of the site is greatly diminished by the railway which runs close to it. But the sad story of Bonnivard, the prisoner of Chillon, and the innumerable poetical associations which cluster around the antique walls, will make it an object of deep and perpetual interest. The interior of the castle well repays a visit. The torture chamber, the beam on

CASTLE OF CHILLON.

which criminals were hung; the *oubliette*, the only entrance to, or exit from which was through a trap-door in the floor above; the dungeons, worn by the pacing to and fro of the prisoners, are all impressive relics of the past. The castle is now used by the canton as a magazine for military stores.

As the end of the lake is approached the hills on either hand subside, and the scenery suffers in proportion. But the change has this compensatory advantage, that it allows of glorious views of Mont Blanc and the Alps of Savoy. Nothing can be more exquisitely beautiful than, at sunset, to look across the waters of the lake to the chain of snowy summits tinged with the delicate flush of evening. The flush of rosy light slowly fading away into cold pure whiteness is quite unearthly in its effect. Near Morges this view may be enjoyed in perfection. Here, too, the mountain may be seen reflected in the lake as in a mighty mirror.

Geneva lies at the foot of the lake, just where the Rhone emerges from it. Most visitors are disappointed in the city. It has neither the picturesque irregularity and air of quaint antiquity which characterises so many continental towns, nor has it attained the gaiety and brilliancy of others which have been modernised, like it, under French influence. A dozen palatial hotels, three or four good streets, a handsome quay, and a maze of dirty lanes, make up the city. The environs, however, are very beautiful; the old ramparts have been turned into agreeable promenades; and the views over the lake, with the distant mountains as a back ground, are magnificent. The Rhone is here an object of especial interest and beauty. It entered the lake turbid and densely charged with the *débris* of the moraines amongst which it has its birth. It emerges translucent in purity, and, in certain conditions of the atmosphere, is almost

GENEVA AND THE RHONE.

indigo in colour. It is photographed in the line which speaks of "The blue rushing of the arrowy Rhone."

Though Geneva is the centre of an admirable system of railway communications, it is one of the few places in which the diligence, which used to be seen lumbering over all the post-roads of the Continent, still lingers. Railroads have not yet penetrated to Chamouni and other parts of Savoy, and communications are maintained by this strange-looking vehicle, of which it is difficult to convey any idea to an English reader. The coupé of a railway carriage, an old-fashioned post-chaise, and a modern omnibus, all joined together, with a Hansom cab, the driver's seat removed from the back to the front, placed upon the top, would perhaps best describe it. The horses, the harness, and the driver baffle description.

Geneva is the capital of the smallest canton in the Confederation. Voltaire, when residing here, used to ridicule its diminutive size by saying, "I shake my periwig and powder the canton." It has, however, exercised an influence altogether out of proportion to its territorial insignificance. This it owes to the

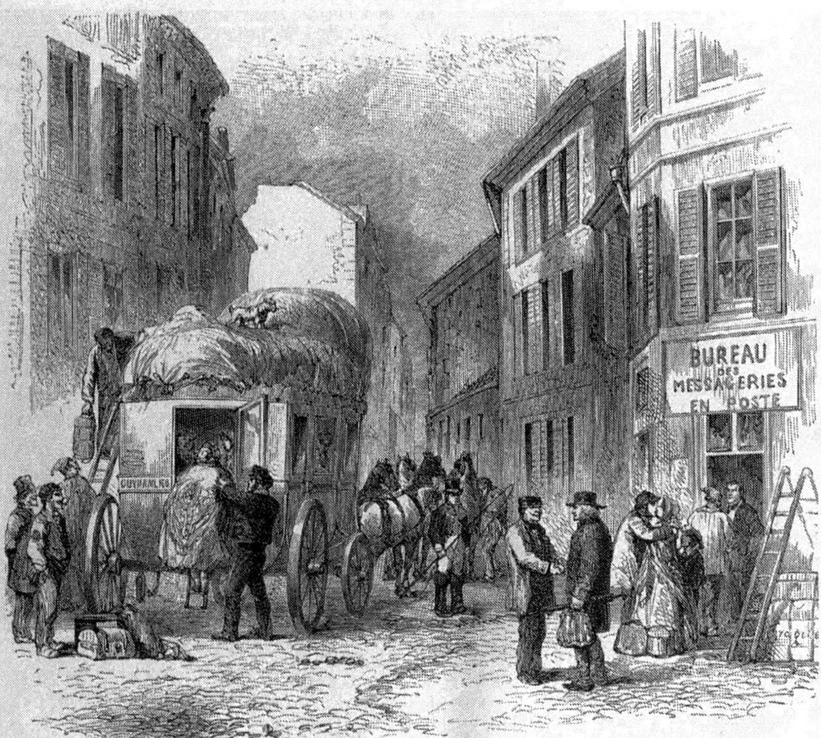

SWISS DILIGENCE.

ennobling and invigorating action of liberty and religion. Up to the time of its complete emancipation from the Dukes of Savoy, it was an obscure and unimportant Swiss town. It cordially embraced the Reformation, shook off the Savoyard yoke, expelled the Catholic bishop, and at once entered upon its brilliant career. In every subsequent generation it has been the birthplace or the adopted home of some of the greatest names in Europe. Calvin, Beza,

Farel, D'Aubigné, Knox, Casaubon, Voltaire, Rousseau, Neckar, Madame de Stael, Saussure, Bonnet, De Luc, De Candolle, Huber, Dumont, Sismondi, are but a few names of those who from Geneva, for good or evil, have exerted a mighty influence upon the world. English Christians will connect it, in more recent times, with the labours of the Haldanes, and with the names of Cæsar Malan, Gaussen, and Merle d'Aubigné. All these have passed away, "and their works do follow them." The eloquent and learned historian of the Reformation survived till October, 1872, to edify the Church, and illustrate her annals.

Calvin, to whom Geneva owes so much, arrived in the city, a fugitive and an exile, in the year 1536. He purposed to remain only a single night, but Farel forcibly detained him, saying, "I declare to you that if you will not remain to help us, the curse of God will rest upon you." These words so impressed themselves on the sensitive mind of Calvin, that he never forgot them. Twenty years afterwards he said, "Those terrible threatenings of Farel were as if God had seized me by His angel's hand from heaven." Thus was Calvin, in his twenty-seventh year, providentially led to Geneva—a place so often and so severely tried in the struggle for political freedom, and which was destined to become a rallying-point in the approaching spiritual revolution. Scarcely could there have been found a spot more fitted for the success of his mission. A free town, in which French was spoken, it was close to the French frontier. True, it was a small, almost an invisible point in the midst of great kingdoms, forming a state containing not more than 20,000 souls. But God judgeth not as man

D'AUBIGNÉ'S BIRTHPLACE AND RESIDENCE.

CALVIN AND FAREL.

"I declare to you, that if you will not remain to help us, the curse of God will rest upon you."

judgeth; He "hath chosen the weak things of the world to confound the things which are mighty; yea, and things which are not, to bring to nought things that are."

When Calvin reached Geneva, he found everything still in disorder, and the city divided into hostile factions. It has been forcibly said that Calvin pursued wickedness with fire and sword, and that his laws were written, not only in blood, but with a pen of flame. His first proceedings in Geneva encountered a fierce resistance. The result was that, in a short time, the preachers were expelled, being ordered to quit the city in three days. Calvin conducted himself on this occasion with much dignity. In the protocol issued April 23rd, the words uttered by him and Farel are recorded to their honour. They must even have inspired their enemies with respect. "Let it be so," say they; "it is better to serve God than man."

Driven thus rudely from Geneva, Calvin retired to Strasbourg, where he resided as in a haven of safety during the next two or three years. After three years' exile, he was restored to Geneva. His heart had remained constantly attached to that city, for whose people he entertained "a singular affection;" nevertheless, when the call came, he shrank back saying, "As often as I think how unhappy I was at Geneva, I tremble, in my innermost being, when mention is made of my return. I know well that, wherever I go, I must always expect to meet with suffering; and that, if I will live for Christ, life must be a conflict." The most urgent efforts were made to induce him to waive all difficulties and comply with the repeated invitations of his former flock. When the Genevese deputies visited Calvin, he could not suppress his feelings: "As I shed more tears than I spoke words," he says, "they entertained no doubt of my sincerity. I was twice compelled to silence and restrain myself. Fain would I have escaped putting my shoulder to the burden; but at length the feeling of duty and faith prevailed, so that I again gave myself to the flock from whom I had been torn. But with how much sorrow! and with how many tears! and with what anguish! God is the best judge of all this." Calvin's motto, as he turned his face again towards Geneva, might have been, like that of St. Paul: "I call God to witness that, if I come again to you, I will not spare."

The 13th of September was the day fixed for Calvin's return to Geneva. The little state was excited and agitated with eager expectation. He was received by the people and magistrates, who, to do him honour, had sent forward a herald to meet him, with every demonstration of affection and triumph. The whole city hailed the event, and so eager were the people to acknowledge themselves the guilty party, that Calvin found it superfluous to deliver the address he had prepared in self-defence. It must have been a stirring spectacle to behold this illustrious man thus re-entering the city, from which he had been so ignominiously expelled, and proceeding, accompanied by an eager throng, to the dwelling prepared for his reception. It was situated at the highest part of the city, with a small garden attached to it, and was not far from the church of St. Peter's, where the Consistory held its meetings, nor from the old church in which he preached and taught. Having installed him with all honour, and presented him with a cloak, the authorities concluded by entreating him, in the most earnest manner, never to leave the city which had thus testified its repentance and attachment.

At this time scarcely any one in Europe exercised greater power in the silent ordering of the events of his age than John Calvin. His influence in England and Scotland was considerable. He wrote to the Protector Somerset, advising him in the management of religious affairs. He subsequently proposed to Cranmer a plan for the general union of the evangelical churches. His influence in the Protestant Church of France was unbounded, and he was regarded with hatred and dread by the French Court, who thirsted for his blood. He held out the hand of fellowship to the Austrian reformed communities, and addressed himself to the reformers of Poland, using every effort to excite the zeal of the great and influential men in that land. His intercourse with Denmark and Sweden was of later date. Beza says, "He bore all these churches on his shoulders."

Queen Mary ascended the British throne in 1553, and Knox, with several other distinguished divines, fled to Switzerland. Calvin was at the acmé of his popularity; his writings were known throughout Europe, and people flocked to him from all parts. He received Knox with cordial welcome; who, in turn, venerated Calvin as a father, and looked to him for counsel and guidance.

Meantime, year after year, he was exercising his office at Geneva, as a preacher of repentance. He had from the first turned his whole attention to the establishment of a court of morals, and with this was closely connected the entire revisal of the laws of the republic. He showed, in the prosecution of these ideas, the resolute and iron will of the man who came forward to restore order and to suppress iniquity. Nor could the fiercest opposition and resistance quell his resolute spirit. He pursued his object throughout his whole life, being willing rather to die than yield.

In truth, it was a giant task he had undertaken. The "gay population of the sweet, joyous wine land," the people who had so long addicted themselves to the fascinations of worldly pleasure, were called on to lay aside these festivities, and to submit to the most rigorous discipline. The city was divided into three parishes, and a watchful eye was kept by the preachers on the families of the citizens. Attendance on preaching and the ordinances was strictly commanded. Irregularities in conduct and morals were punished with a stern severity which startles and revolts one's spirit. Alas! that the fiery zeal of Calvin did not restrict itself to the punishment of profligacy and crime. In an evil day, the pile was kindled that consumed Servetus, and thus brought a scandal on his name which no lapse of time can obliterate, and gave occasion to the enemies of God's truth to blaspheme.

As soon as Charles IX. ascended the throne of France, a letter was addressed to the Council at Geneva by Queen Catherine, stating that the king and his states declared that all the disturbances in France had been occasioned by the preachers sent thither from Geneva. It was required that these teachers should be recalled, and "none others like them be sent. Else would the king be justified in taking vengeance on a city which was undermining his state."

The Romanists had, indeed, reason to bestir themselves; for through the influence exerted by Calvin in promoting the diffusion of the new faith, it was estimated that, looking to France alone, there were five millions who professed the reformed doctrines. Beza relates that, immediately after the conference of Poissy (1561), the Queen sent to number the churches, and there were 2150. At this juncture, peace was looked for, and the reformed religion seemed to be on the point of triumphing. The Church in Paris flourished, and the numerous persons of distinction who belonged to it were desirous of calling Calvin to their assistance. But the Council of Geneva would not part with him, nor was he disposed to leave the little republic.

High as Calvin now stood, there were not wanting things to humble him. His health, so long frail, now began entirely to give way. Yet he laboured even

MEMORIAL HALL OF THE REFORMATION, GENEVA.

more abundantly; and his efforts, literary, epistolary, and ministerial, were perfectly astonishing. He was never happier, according to his own statement, than when he was obliged to do many and important things. He also took part in the concerns of the city itself, as we learn from his zealous exertions during the plague; and when, in 1559, the citizens were threatened with a siege, he set an example to them, by uniting with the professors and preachers in labouring at the fortifications. His whole life was intensely earnest, and even in his later years his soul never became, in the least degree, enfeebled or troubled. One feeling governed him—the feeling of duty, for which alone he lived; and his care for souls was a burning zeal that never slackened. He was always striving to save souls, to keep alive the consciousness of sin and the necessity of salvation, because, said he, "for every single soul the preacher must give account." In the year 1558 Calvin was attacked by a violent fever, which bowed him down. He now, for the first time, began to feel old; and the sigh which occasionally escaped him told of the internal distress. "It might be clearly seen," says Beza, "that he was hastening by rapid strides to a better world. Yet he could not be induced to spare himself, and ceased not to comfort the afflicted, to exhort, to preach, and to lecture. 'Would you that the Lord should find me idle when He comes?' was his answer, when we besought him to refrain. The year 1564 was the first of his eternal rest, and the beginning, for us, of a long and justifiable grief."

Calvin preached his last sermon on the 6th of February. A violent fit of coughing cut short his discourse, and he was supported out of the church. Three weeks later he repaired to the council-chamber, leaning on two friends, and, taking off his skull-cap, spoke a few words to the assembly, thanking them for the kindness he had experienced at their hands, and adding his farewell; "for I feel," said he, "that this is the last time I shall stand here."

On the 2nd of April, being Easter Sunday, he was carried to church, where he received the communion from the hands of Beza, who tells how, with a trembling voice, his dying friend joined the congregation in the last hymn, "Lord, let thy servant depart in peace." This was his last appearance in public. His weakness increased rapidly, paralysis seized his head and right side, and at the request of his friends he made his will. He died poor. So great was his disinterestedness, that the sceptic Bayle, after saying that he left behind him property worth only 300 crowns, could not withhold an exclamation of wonder. "This," says he, "is one of the most uncommon victories that the virtue and grandeur of a powerful mind can gain over nature, even in those who exercise the gospel ministry." Yet, during his life the most absurd rumours were circulated as to his wealth, and he had more than once to defend himself against these slanders. At length he exclaimed, "My death will prove what they would not believe in my life."

A short time before his decease, the members of the council were admitted to an interview with their dying pastor. His strength rallied when they came into the room, and he addressed them at some length, recapitulating the many and arduous struggles in which they had been engaged together, the dangers they had shared, and the blessings they had received. He concluded by praising the boundless mercy of God, and His goodness poured so richly upon all; and besought them to pursue their future course with foresight, and in the fear of the Lord, hiding themselves under His wings. "You know," he said, "I am myself the best evidence of His power to save. The Lord so strengthened me alway, that, fearful and weak as I was by nature, by His aid I have overcome all enemies without and within." What words are these to be uttered by a dying believer! Such farewell testimonies to the goodness, fidelity, and power of our God and Saviour are the best legacies bequeathed to the church in all ages.

ANNECY.

He lingered on till the 28th of May, when he gently expired in the arms of Beza, being then in the 54th year of his age. According to his express desire, his funeral was conducted in the most unostentatious manner; and in compliance with his request, the Genevese raised no monument to his memory, nor marked his grave with a stone. Save the house in which he lived, No. 116 Rue des Chanoines, a large number of MSS. in the museum, and a few personal relics, such as his chair and part of his pulpit in the cathedral, Geneva possesses no material relics of her great reformer. But his influence was spiritual and intellectual. He left his mark upon the mind of the people. The history of the city is his noblest monument.

Amongst the other religious refugees from France who have sought and found a shelter in Geneva and its neighbourhood, we meet with Madame Guyon. On the death of her husband she was strongly urged to retire to Annecy, and there engage, without hindrance, in the service of her Lord and Master. Acting upon this advice, she left Paris, and reached her destination, about twenty miles from Geneva, on 22nd of July, 1681. On the next day, at the tomb of St. Francis de Sales, she renewed the consecration of herself to Christ, and forthwith entered upon her self-imposed task. She took up her residence at Gex, near Geneva, and

NEFF SETTING OUT TO PREACH.

engaged in visiting the sick and poor, teaching the ignorant, and reclaiming the sinful. Soon afterwards she removed to Thonon, on the shores of the lake. Her reputation for piety and charity had preceded her. All day long her room was filled with inquirers, "her little children," as she called them. She seems to have been the means of pointing many to Christ, and leading them to find in Him the peace and satisfaction they had vainly sought before. After remaining at Thonon for some time the priests became alarmed at the influence she was gaining, and the success that attended her labours. They set themselves, therefore, to drive her away; assailing her with odious charges, and burning her books in public. At length they procured an order from the bishop commanding her to leave his diocese. Sorrowfully she obeyed, and retired to Turin.

Amongst the great and good men whose names illustrate the Genevese annals in modern times, that of Felix Neff should not be forgotten. He was born in a village near the city in the year 1798. Twenty years later he was "born again" in the city itself. And thither in ten years more he returned to die. Yet in those ten short years how much of intense and devoted labour was crowded! Measuring life by years, we mourn over the premature death of the youth who passes away at thirty. Measuring life by labour and achievement, he had attained a good old age. Few men have done more during a lifetime than he in the brief interval between his conversion and his departure. Of the nature of those labours the following extract from one of his own letters may serve as an illustration. "I preached," says Neff, "on the sabbath at Dormilleuse, and early next morning took my departure, in order to cross the Col d'Orsière, a mountain which separates the valley of Fressinière from that of Champsaur, through which the river Drac runs. I had two guides to direct me in crossing this mountain. At this season of the year the passage is seldom practicable. Having left the village of Dormilleuse, we proceeded onwards towards the Col, along the foot of the glaciers, walking for three hours through snows, some of which had recently fallen, but the greater part probably had lain for centuries. The sky was clear and beautiful, and, notwithstanding our great elevation, the cold was not unusually severe. In many places the snow was firm, but in others quite soft, and we often sank in it up to our knees. The peasants had, however, been considerate enough to envelope my shoes with wool; and we had furnished ourselves with a plentiful supply of provisions for our journey. Since the fall of snow in September, only two persons had effected this passage, and we followed in their track, which was crossed at intervals by the footmarks of wolves and chamois, and traces of marmot-hunters. After we had gained the summit of the Col, we had still the prospect of a dreary walk of two hours, before we could reach the first hamlet of the Val d'Orsière, lying at the foot of the snows, near the sources of the Drac. Here my guides left me, and I proceeded alone towards Mens."

In the month of January (1824) Neff writes: "Last sabbath, I preached twice at Violin, after which I retired to a cottage, where I read a portion of Scripture, and commented upon it, until ten at night, when my congregation withdrew. Many of them had come from remote distances, and as the night was dark, they provided themselves with torches to guide them through the snow. The next morning I began my ascent towards Dormilleuse, the last and most elevated of all the hamlets in the valley of Fressinière. Its inhabitants, descended in an unbroken line from the ancient Vaudois, have rendered it celebrated by their resistance, during six hundred years, to the efforts of the Church of Rome. Their brethren in some of the adjacent communes, whose habitations were not so guarded by rugged ramparts and precipices, were often surprised by their foes, and compelled either to dissemble their faith or become the victims of cruel persecution. Many of them fled to Dormilleuse, where they found an impregnable refuge. This place stands upon the brink of a rock, which is almost perpendicular; it is completely surrounded by glaciers; and a dark forest stretches along the flank of the mountain, presenting a striking contrast to the snow which covers its summit. The only place where the ascent is practicable is a steep and slippery footpath. A mere handful of men stationed here could with ease repel the attacks of a numerous army, and hurl their assailants into the frightful abyss beneath. For six hundred years Dormilleuse was the city of refuge for the Christians of these valleys, who had successfully resisted both violence and seduction, and, during this long period, had never crouched before the idols of the Church of Rome, or suffered their religion to be tainted by any of its corruptions. There are yet visible the ruins of the walls and fortresses which they erected to preserve themselves from surprise, and to repel the frequent assaults of their oppressors. The sublime yet frightful aspect of this mountain desert, which

CHÂLET IN THE MOUNTAINS.

served as a retreat for the truth, when nearly the whole world was shrouded in darkness; the remembrance of so many martyrs whose blood once bedewed its rocks; the deep caverns to which they resorted for the purpose of reading the Holy Scriptures, and worshipping the eternal God in spirit and in truth—the sight of all these tends to elevate the soul, and to inspire one with feelings which are difficult to be expressed."

Lausanne is second only to Geneva as a centre of intellectual life for

LAUSANNE, AND THE LAKE OF GENEVA.

Switzerland. The railway from the one city to the other runs along the northern bank of the lake, and affords a series of magnificent views, which some prefer even to those enjoyed upon the lake itself. The traveller, moving upon a higher level, commands a wider landscape, a broader expanse of water is beneath his eye, and the snowy peaks of Savoy and the Valais are more constantly above the horizon. The views from the lake and the railway are, both of them, so varied and so interesting, that it seems invidious to disparage either in the comparison with the other. Lausanne stands finely upon the lower slopes of Mont Jorat as it sinks down to the lake. From the higher parts of the town, especially from the terrace of the cathedral, noble views of the lake and distant mountains are gained. The town itself is tortuous and picturesque, now sinking down a ravine and now climbing a height, the old streets with high-piled houses wander up and down, whilst the castle and cathedral keep watch over their time-hallowed precincts. A circle of beauty girdles round this mass of grey, irregular buildings—pleasant country walks, park-like scenery, well-kept vineyards, and the ample gardens of country houses, with lawn and shrubbery, fountains and flowers. Beyond this stretches the lake, once surrounded by thick forests, and obscured by the dense fogs that brooded over it; now its shores are fringed with villas and towns which have become familiar names throughout Europe and America.

Amongst the innumerable literary associations which cluster round Lausanne, one of the most interesting is that connected with the conclusion of Gibbon's great work, *The Decline and Fall of the Roman Empire.* Its preparation had been the task of years, it may be said of a lifetime, for to it were devoted the vast stores of learning accumulated throughout his life. In his autobiography, Gibbon records the completion of this monument of unsurpassed erudition : "It was on the day, or rather night, of the 27th of June, 1787, between the hours of eleven and twelve, that I wrote the last lines of the last page in a summer-house in my garden. After laying down my pen, I took several turns in a *berceau*, or covered walk of acacias, which commands a prospect of the country, the lake, and the mountains. The air was temperate, the sky was serene, the silver orb of the moon was reflected from the waters, and all nature was silent. I will not dissemble the first emotions of joy on recovery of my freedom, and perhaps the establishment of my fame. But my pride was soon humbled, and a sober melancholy was spread over my mind by the idea that I had taken an everlasting leave of an old and agreeable companion, and that whatsoever might be the future of my history, the life of the historian must be short and precarious."

From Lausanne to Neufchâtel there is little to detain the tourist. The railway winds round the lower spurs and slopes of the Jura, amongst solemn pine-woods interchanging with rich pastures and trim vineyards ; whilst the lakes of Geneva and Neufchâtel add brightness to the scene. The scenery of the Jura is seldom appreciated as highly as it deserves to be. The tourist is either hurrying forward to enjoy the grander views which await him a day's journey onward, or he is returning, his eyes sated, his mind wearied by sublimity and beauty. And the Jura does not disclose its characteristic beauties to the passing tourist, who posts over the main routes with feverish haste, and demands something sensational to arrest his wandering glance. But he who knows how to reap "the harvest of a quiet eye ;" he who can patiently and peacefully commune with Nature in her gentler moods, will find in these solemn pine-woods and mountain slopes and bright pastures a peculiar charm. It is of this district that Mr. Ruskin writes in his *Seven Lamps of Architecture* :

"It is a spot which has all the solemnity, with none of the savageness, of the Alps ; where there is a sense of a great power beginning to be manifested in the earth, and of a deep and majestic concord in the rise of the long low lines of piny hills ; the first utterance of those mighty mountain symphonies, soon to be more loudly lifted and wildly broken along the battlements of the Alps. But their strength is as yet restrained ; and the far-reaching ridges of pastoral mountain succeed each other, like the long and sighing swell which moves over quiet waters from some far-off stormy sea. And there is a deep tenderness pervading that vast monotony. The destructive forces and the stern expression of the central ranges are alike withdrawn. No frost-ploughed, dust-encumbered

NEUFCHÂTEL.

paths of ancient glacier fret the soft Jura pastures; no splintered heaps of ruin break the fair ranks of her forests; no pale, defiled, or furious rivers rend their rude and changeful ways among her rocks. Patiently, eddy by eddy, the clear green streams wind along their well-known beds; and under the dark quietness of the undisturbed pines, there spring up, year by year, such a company of joyful flowers as I know not the like of among all the blessings of the earth. It was spring time, too; and all were coming forth in clusters crowded for very love; there was room enough for all, but they crushed their leaves into all manner of strange shapes only to be nearer each other. . . . I came out presently on the edge of the ravine: the solemn murmur of its waters rose suddenly from beneath, mixed with the singing of the thrushes among the pine boughs; and on the opposite side of the valley, walled all along as it was by grey cliffs of limestone, there was a hawk sailing slowly off their brow, touching them nearly with his wings, and with the shadows of the pines flickering upon his plumage from above; but with a fall of a hundred fathoms under his breast, and the curling pools of the green river gliding and glittering dizzily beneath him, their foam globes moving with him as he flew. It would be difficult to conceive a scene less dependent upon any other interest than that of its own secluded and serious beauty; but the writer well remembers the sudden blankness and chill which were cast upon it when he endeavoured, in order more strictly to arrive at the sources of its impressiveness, to imagine it, for a moment, a scene in some aboriginal forest of the New Continent. The flowers in an instant lost their light, the river its music; the hills became oppressively desolate; a heaviness in the boughs of the darkened forest showed how much of their former power had been dependent upon a life which was not theirs, how much of the glory of the imperishable, or continually renewed, creation is reflected from things more precious in their memories than it, in its renewing. Those ever springing flowers and ever flowing streams had been dyed by the deep colours of human endurance, valour, and virtue; and the crests of the sable hills that rose against the evening sky received a deeper worship, because their far shadows fell eastward over the iron wall of Joux and the four-square keep of Granson."

GAP, THE BIRTHPLACE OF FAREL.

The main instrument in carrying forward the Reformation in the city and canton of Neufchâtel was William Farel. Born at Gap, in the High Alps, he early distinguished himself at the University of Paris, and was made Regent of the College founded by Cardinal le Moine—a post which had always been filled by men of eminence. Embracing the doctrines of the Reformation, he had to fly from France and take refuge in Switzerland. Basle, Zurich, Berne, and Geneva shared in his apostolic labours. But it is with Neufchâtel that his name is especially connected. His uncompromising fidelity and impetuous zeal repeatedly stirred up such a spirit of hostility against himself that he had to fly from the city. But he was always recalled and received with distinguished honour. He lived to see the enemies of the gospel in Neufchâtel reduced to silence, and the whole canton united in the profession of Protestantism. At the age of seventy-five he walked from Neufchâtel to Geneva, to bid farewell to his beloved friend Calvin, who was on his death-bed. He only survived the great Genevese reformer fifteen months, gently falling asleep on the 13th September, 1565. His earliest biographer and attached friend, Faber, says of him :—"Without lessening the praise and commendation due to the labours of others, the zeal, activity, and devotedness of Farel, both in advancing the Reformation and in preaching the gospel, place him in the very first rank." He was buried on the Minster terrace, where a monument testifies to the gratitude and affection of the citizens.

With Neufchâtel our Swiss tour terminates. But surely it cannot terminate without an ascription of praise to Him who "by His strength setteth fast the mountains being girded with power."

"Bless the Lord, O my soul.
O Lord my God, thou art very great; thou art clothed with honour and majesty.
Who coverest thyself with light as with a garment:
Who stretchest out the heavens like a curtain:
Who layeth the beams of his chambers in the waters:
Who maketh the clouds his chariot: who walketh upon the wings of the wind:
Who maketh his angels spirits; his ministers a flaming fire:
Who laid the foundations of the earth, that it should not be removed for ever. . . .
The glory of the Lord shall endure for ever:
The Lord shall rejoice in his works.
He looketh on the earth, and it trembleth:
He toucheth the hills, and they smoke.
I will sing unto the Lord as long as I live:
I will sing praise to my God while I have my being.
My meditation of him shall be sweet: I will be glad in the Lord."

Psalm civ.

HOME AGAIN!

HEIGHT ABOVE THE SEA OF THE PRINCIPAL MOUNTAINS AND PASSES MENTIONED IN THIS VOLUME.

MOUNTAINS.

	Eng. Feet.		*Eng. Feet.*		*Eng. Feet.*
Mont Blanc	15,784	Breithorn	13,685	Gorner-Grat	10,290
Monte Rosa	15,223	Jungfrau	13,671	Æggischorn	9,657
Dom	14,935	Shreckhorn	13,394	Brévent	8,380
Lyskamm	14,889	Wetterhorn	12,166	Niesen	7,765
Weisshorn	14,804	Blümlis Alp	12,041	Pilatus	7,315
Matterhorn	14,705	Diablerets	10,666	Flegère	6,250
Finsteraarhorn	14,039	Titlis	10,634	Rigi	5,905
Aletschhorn	13,803				

PASSES.

Weissthor	11,851	St. Bernard	8,120	Col de Balme	7,231
Col du Géant	11,196	Furca	8,000	Splugen	6,945
St. Théodule	10,899	Surenen	7,578	St. Gothard	6,936
Monte Moro	9,390	Gemmi	7,540	Cenis	6,773
Col de la Seigne	8,300	Susten	7,440	Wengern Alp	6,690
Col du Bonhomme	8,195	Joch	7,340	Simplon	6,628

POPULATION OF THE SWISS CANTONS IN DECEMBER 1870.

CANTONS.	*Protestants.*	*Roman Catholics.*	*Jews.*	*Others.*	*Total.*
Aargau	107,720	89,180	1,542	432	198,874
Appenzell	46,377	14,084	21	166	60,648
Basle	77,980	22,552	647	716	101,895
Berne	436,446	66,007	1,401	2,707	506,561
Fribourg	16,805	94,027	50	15	110,897
Geneva	44,138	48,340	1,001	637	94,116
Glaris	28,230	6,896	17	7	35,150
Grisons	51,886	39,855	18	35	91,794
Lucerne	3,837	128,337	98	65	132,337
Neufchâtel	84,357	11,329	674	926	97,286
Schaffhausen	34,466	3,051	24	180	37,721
Schwytz	642	47,054	7	4	47,707
Solure	12,448	62,078	93	99	74,718
St. Gall	74,589	116,130	192	185	191,096
Thurgau	69,229	23,456	84	539	93,308
Ticino	192	119,300	30	47	119,569
Unterwalden	430	25,678	5	0	26,113
Uri	80	16,019	8	1	16,108
Valais	904	96,154	4	19	97,081
Vaud	211,581	17,530	601	1,794	231,506
Zug	878	20,083	15	17	20,993
Zurich	263,788	17,944	505	2,630	284,867
Total	1,567,003	1,085,084	7,037	11,221	2,670,345

CHRONOLOGICAL TABLE.

110 B.C.—The Tigurini, a Helvetic tribe under Divico, invade Gaul: they defeat the Roman consul, L. Cassius, who, with Piso, his lieutenant, and an immense number of men, were left dead upon the field. The Tigurini and their allies, the Cimbri, advance into Italy, but are repulsed with great slaughter by Marius.

60–58 B.C.—The Tigurini and other Helvetic tribes led by Divico, their former commander, resolve to establish themselves in Gaul. Three years are occupied in preparation; 368,000 men, women, and children set out. They are attacked and repulsed by Julius Cæsar. Only 100,000 survive to return to their homes. Roman garrisons are established in several strategic points of Helvetia, and a fortress constructed at Noviodunum (Nyon), on the Lake of Geneva.

50 B.C.–800 A.D.—For the next three or four centuries the Helvetii remained subject to Rome, with only occasional and partial attempts at insurrection. On the irruption of the Northern hordes, various tribes settled in Helvetia. The Burgundians established themselves on the slopes of the Jura, on the shores of the Lake of Geneva, and the lower Valley of the Rhone. The Allemanni occupied what is now known as the Bernese Oberland and North-eastern Switzerland. The Goths settled in the district of the Pennine Alps. The Franks subsequently conquered Helvetia under Charlemagne. On the breaking up of the Carlovingian empire, Helvetia was dismembered. In the course of the fifth century the Burgundians were converted to Christianity. Two centuries later Columbanus, an Irish monk, led a party of missionaries from Gaul into the district occupied by the Allemanni. They were successful, not only in preaching the gospel, but in introducing agriculture and civilisation.

889.—Rudolf, Count of Burgundy, is recognised as king by the lords and bishops assembled at St. Maurice.

919.—Helvetia being ravaged by the Huns, the Emperor Henry I. encourages the formation of fortified towns as places of retreat and defence. Hence spring up Zurich, St. Gall, Fribourg, Berne, Basle, and other cities.

1218.—Frederick II. grants imperial charters to Berne, Soleure, Basle, and Schaffhausen.

1273.—Rudolf of Hapsburg, a wealthy and influential nobleman of Aargau and Schwytz, is chosen Emperor of Germany. He favours the establishment, and enlarges the privileges, of the free cities.

1291.—Rudolf dies, and is succeeded by his son Albert, who, pursuing an opposite policy, alienates the affections of his Swiss subjects.

1300–1308.—The Forest Cantons resolve to throw off the yoke of the House of Hapsburg. Gessler is appointed imperial bailiff. He is resisted by William Tell, who unites with Werner Stauffacher, Walter Furst, and Arnold von Melchthal in a solemn oath to liberate their country. Tell kills Gessler; an insurrection breaks out, the Austrians are driven away, and their castles razed to the ground.

1315.—Leopold of Austria is defeated at Morgarten in his attempt to re-establish the authority of the Hapsburgs. A Federal pact is agreed upon amongst the inhabitants of the Forest Cantons. Schwytz being the most important amongst them, the name of Schwytzers comes into use for all the confederates: hence Swiss and Switzerland.

1332.—Lucerne joins the confederation of the Waldstätter.

1351–1352.—Zurich, Glarus, Zug, and Berne join the Confederation.

1386.—Leopold III. attacks Lucerne: is defeated and slain at Sempach.

1389.—The Austrians having suffered successive defeats, consent to make peace with the Confederation.

1415.—The Council of Constance is held; Frederick of Austria being excommunicated by the Council, the Swiss invade and annex Aargau.

1418–1424.—The Swiss invade the Italian valleys and form them into bailiwicks. The Valaisians revolt against their feudal lord and form an alliance with the Confederacy. The Graubund or Grison league is formed.

1452.—War between the Confederation and Austria; Rapperschwyl, Fribourg, and Thurgau wrested from Austria. A few years later, Sigismund sells to the Confederation the last remaining possessions of Austria in Switzerland, including even the castle of Hapsburg itself.

1475–1476.—War between the Burgundians and Swiss; the former are defeated with immense slaughter at Granson and Morat.

1481.—Dissensions break out between the several cantons respecting the admission of Fribourg and Soleure into the Confederacy, and civil war seems imminent. The exertions of Nicholas von der Flue avert the catastrophe, and they are peaceably admitted.

1499.—Maximilian I., being defeated by the Swiss, makes peace, and virtually acknowledges their independence.

1501.—Basle and Schaffhausen are admitted into the Confederacy. Twelve years later Appenzell is admitted, completing the thirteen cantons of which Switzerland consisted up to the time of the French Revolution; Geneva, Neufchâtel, the Valais, and the Grisons being independent allied republics.

1518–1519.—Zwingle, Bullinger, and others assail the doctrines of the Church of Rome.

1523–1530.—Zurich, Berne, Basle, Schaffhausen, and Neufchâtel adopt the doctrines of the Reformation. Many other cities and cantons do so in part.

1531–1537.—Farel and Calvin preach the gospel at Geneva. The Genevese rise against the Duke of Savoy and expel their Bishop. The Bernese support the Genevese, and take the Pays de Vaud from the Duke of Savoy.

1544.—The Grisons join the Swiss Confederacy as allies.

1603.—The Duke of Savoy acknowledges the independence of Geneva.

1621–1639.—Invasion of the Grisons by the Austrians. The French aid the Swiss in driving out the invaders.

1648.—The independence of the Swiss Confederation recognised by the European powers in the treaty of Westphalia.

1653–1712.—A succession of internal feuds and civil wars caused by the resistance of the peasantry to the tyranny of their masters, or arising out of the religious dissensions between Catholics and Protestants.

1713–1792.—A period of peace for Switzerland.

1793–1800.—The French revolutionary government foment dissensions amongst the Swiss, invade Switzerland, are resisted by some of the cantons and supported by others. The Austrians and Russians enter Switzerland to oppose the French; a period of general confusion follows.

1815.—The allied Powers, at the Congress of Vienna, recognise the independence of Switzerland and establish the Federal pact.

www.ingramcontent.com/pod-product-compliance
Ingram Content Group UK Ltd.
Pitfield, Milton Keynes, MK11 3LW, UK
UKHW021258100625
6297UKWH00063B/73

9 781013 748271